Praying and Proclaiming

God's Abundant PROVISION

Effectual Fervent Prayers and Proclamations of Faith for God's Abundant Provision

By Joel Hitchcock

Copyright Information:

ISBN-13: 978-1545237908
ISBN-10: 1545237905

Dedication

I dedicate this book to my wife and best friend Heidi, who it the greatest woman of faith in God's provision I know. Honey, God truly handpicked you for me. Our journey of faith has been an exciting one, and God has always provided in all our needs, even when we did not know where it would come from next.

And to my children – Anthony, Rebekah, Timothy and Trey: As ministers' kids you have learnt to live the life of faith in God's provision. You have seen the Lord supply in all our need according to his riches in glory by Christ Jesus (Philippians 4:19.) And kids, God will always provide for you – just keep on trusting Him and you will see God intervene for you in supernatural ways.

And to those many wonderful friends and supporters of our ministry – you have believed in us and in what we do. You have supported us with your sacrificial giving. We are indebted to you, our friends. With your support we have pulled off some big things for the kingdom of God. You remind me of our Lord's own supporters:

“Soon afterward Jesus began a tour of the nearby towns and villages, preaching and announcing the Good News about the kingdom of God. He took his twelve disciples with him, along with … many others who were contributing from their own resources to support Jesus and his disciples” (Luke 8:1-3, NLT.)

And finally to my Lord and Savior, the King of kings and Lord of lords – who loved me and gave Himself for me (Galatians 2:20, ULKJV.) You are Jehovah Jireh – the LORD my Provider (Genesis 22:14.) You have given me the desires of my heart (Psalm 37:4.)

Praying and Proclaiming God's Abundant PROVISION

Effectual Fervent Prayers and Proclamations of Faith for God's Abundant Provision

By Joel Hitchcock

Prosperity Prayer Points (Contents)

God's Will is Prosperity

This book is power packed with promises from the Word of God regarding the **prosperity** and **abundant provision** God intends for his people. These Scriptures on **prosperity** and **abundance** are written in prayer form.

By reading them silently or out loud you will be communicating with the God of the Bible – the God who has bound Himself in covenant with us, and who will honor his side.

As a preacher of the Gospel, I have had to claim these promises many times. You see, I have been a minister of the Gospel and a missionary evangelist for many years and have not had the financial resources of the powers that be.

I had to turn to the Bible and see what God said about my daily sustenance. Did God intend for me to always be in lack?

Would He meet my need? Was He limited to only meeting my needs, or could He do more than that since I was his child?

The focus of my ministry has always been and continues to be more so on salvation,[1] healing & miracles,[2] the Holy Spirit,[3] Christ in me,[4] and about the very Person of God.[5] I have also diligently studied the Scriptures that deal with God's material **provision** for his children.

These Scriptures have been a comfort to me in trying times, and I have come to learn to trust my God every step of the way for my financial **provision**. God has been faithful.

The more these truths became real in my soul, the more I became aware of the lack of faith that many of us have when it comes to God's **abundant provision**. For example, when I preach on this topic, oftentimes to my amazement it seems that many of

---

[1] See author's book, *One Almighty Mediator* and *The Great King and the Little Ant,* available at www.joelhitchcock.blogspot.com

[2] See author's book, M*iracles for the Multitudes – the Miracle Ministry of Signs and Wonders,* available at www.joelhitchcock.blogspot.com.

[3] See author's videos on the Holy Spirit at www.YouTube.com/c/joelhitchcock

available at www.joelhitchcock.blogspot.com

[4] See author's book, *Christ in you,* for great truths regarding the dwelling of Christ within the believer, available at www.joelhitchcock.blogspot.com

[5] See author's book, *Son of God and Man – the deity and humanity of Jesus Christ,* and *Jehovah Incarnate – the Identity of Jesus Christ,* available at www.joelhitchcock.blogspot.com

God's people just cannot get themselves to believe these promises of God.

Therefore, I compiled these Scriptures in such a way that it could be *prayed and proclaimed* out loud. By so doing, the people of God could pray the pure Word of God as it relates to his **provision**—not man's ideas, but God's Word on the subject.

Like the apostle Paul, I have experienced both lack and **abundance**, but through it all I have learnt that I can do all things through Christ who strengthens me (see Philippians 4:11-13.)

I have seen God's hand of **provision** when someone stuck $50 in mine after I gave my last penny in an offering during a revival.[6] I've also seen his hand of **provision** in action when someone sent our ministry $40,000 to hold two soul winning, healing campaigns in which multitudes received Christ and healing.[7]

I have also come to learn that the devil, the enemy of our souls seems to also have a very special interest in the financial destruction of God's people. He either fights them with poverty, lack

[6]The word "revival" here is used in the sense of being special worship services marked with evangelistic preaching and ministry intended to "revive" or renew the faith of God's people. For more information about revival in the sense of a sovereign move of God, and broader spiritual great awakening, see the author's book *Young Fire – Youth Revivalists for the Great Awakening*, available at www.joelhitchcock.blogspot.com.

[7] See pictures of the multitudes in the photo section of this book.

and scarcity, or he fights them by offering them **wealth** and **riches** in *his* world.

Many sincere Bible teachers have at times perhaps praised the virtues of poverty and by so doing negated the great promises of God for **prosperity** and his **abundant provision**.

And yet others have perhaps overly praised the virtues of **prosperity** and **wealth**, as if it was the main message of Christianity, and by so doing negated the more important messages such as the atonement and union with God through the death and resurrection of Christ.

What I have come to learn, beyond a shadow of a doubt is that *our God is a good God*: He is a God of love, and a God who also takes a very special interest in the material wellbeing of his people. As our Heavenly Father, He has the highest ideals for his children. Our God is a better Father to us, than the most loving earthly fathers could ever be to their children after the flesh.

God's Word says, "If you all then … know how to give good gifts unto your children, how much more shall your Father which is in heaven give good things to them that ask Him? (Matthew 7:11, ULKJV.)

He wants us to ask of Him, for we have not because we ask not (James 4:3.) He also wants us to speak things into existence by *declaring it by faith*:

his Word says, "Have faith in God. For verily I say unto you, that whosoever shall say unto this mountain, you be removed, and you be cast into the sea; and shall not doubt in his heart, but shall believe that those things which he says shall come to pass; he shall have whatsoever he says" (Mark 11:22-23, ULKJV.)

It is of the utmost importance that such declarations and requests be made in accordance *with the will of God.* his will is not some vague, mysterious idea that man has no insight into. Rather, his will is clearly revealed in his Word. The Scriptures as we find them in the Bible are inspired by the Holy Spirit and contain the very Words of the Almighty God! When we pray the *Word of God* we pray the *will of God.*

For this reason, I have compiled these *effectual, fervent prayers for* **prosperity** *and* **abundant provision**. These prayers are actually *the Word in prayer form*, enriched with God's promises and filled with the Spirit.

I cannot think of any prayers that can be more powerful than the Word of God in prayer form, filled with the Holy Spirit and faith. Having said that, I also know that at times all we can do is to just *cry out to God* in the midst of our trials. The God of mercy hears us and knows our needs before they even occur.

Another benefit to praying the Word is that continuous exposure to his promises, focused on a certain subject, will build your faith in that specific area – much like when exercising a specific muscle would build that muscle.

Scripture teaches us, "So then faith comes by hearing, and hearing by the word of God" (Romans 10:17, ULKJV.)

It is important to understand that God is a God of *covenant.* "Covenant" means that He has gifted us with agreements of commands and promises. As we obey his commands, He responds by fulfilling his promises. Yes, God is sovereign, but it is He Himself that chose to give us promises that we will benefit from when we obey Him.

For example, this Scripture clearly shows the relation of **blessing** and obedience: *"If you all are willing and obedient, you all shall eat the good of the land (Isaiah 1:19,* ULKJV.*)* There it is: If we do this, then He will do that. God is a God of covenant.

It is a wonderful thing that the Sovereign God gave man the power to choose to be obedient and enjoy his **blessings**. It is true with salvation: We have to choose to receive Him. It is true with healing: It is by faith that we receive it. The same with the baptism in the Holy Spirit – this too is received by faith.

God does not get manipulated by our prayers. Rather, He has presented us with a covenant: He commands and He promises, and we obey and receive the fulfillment of those promises.

I may also note that I have compiled these prayers directly from the Scriptures, and believe that tremendous confidence results from the knowledge that what we pray is God's will because it is in his Word. However, some of these prayers should be viewed in the context in which those specific Scriptures were written, such as the ones about Job who had been the **wealthiest** man in the East.

Obviously, not everyone can be the **wealthiest** in their geographical location, but Job's example may serve as an encouragement and as a challenge to believe that God would **supply** unto us his **abundant blessing** and **provision**, and make us more effective in our own realm of influence. With this in mind, we may pray and believe God for his very best, and glean from examples of those who were **blessed** with the very best in Bible times.

Ask yourself this question: What is the main reason why God would want to bless me with **prosperity** and **abundant provision**? By answering this question, the intents of our hearts are revealed. Is it to retire comfortably? Is it to build a big house and drive a couple of shiny cars? Is it to take a vacation to any place in the world, do it as often as we wish and stay as long as we want? God is at work in our lives – purifying our motives, building our character and steering our passions to God and his kingdom.

Of course it's not wrong or evil to build a big house, drive a shiny car or enjoy a nice vacation. But life does not consist in the things we possess, and he who dies with the most toys is not the winner.

So what is the main reason why God wants to bless you with **wealth** and **riches**? It is to advance the kingdom of our Lord Jesus Christ. Oh yes, it is also because He is just so good and He wants to bless his kids. And yes, it is also because He revels in fulfilling his covenant promises. But the main reason for **abundant provision** is and should be to advance the kingdom of God.

Ask yourself another question: If you were the devil, what would you want for God's children? Would you want them **prospering** and advancing the kingdom of God? Or would you rather want to keep God's people in financial bondage, unable to fund missions work and building God's kingdom locally?

I think he will either distract God's people with the love of money, or he will want to deprive them of financial soundness and force them into subjection to lack and scarcity. This way they will be completely impotent and powerless, ineffective and unable to advance and fund the Gospel and the kingdom of God.

It is my sincere prayer that *Jehovah Jireh* – the Lord our **Provider**) will hear these prayers for your benefit and also stir and strengthen your faith for spiritual as well as material **prosperity** and **abundant provision**.

Enter into Covenant with God

All the **blessings** that we may receive from God are founded on *the* greatest **blessing** – Jesus Christ. If you have never accepted Christ as your savior, or if you perhaps wish to reaffirm your faith in Him, please first pray the "Prayer of Salvation – Receive Christ and Eternal Life" at the end of this book.

The Effectual Fervent Prayer of the Righteous

Before we pray the Scriptures specifically related to **prosperity** and God's **abundant provision**, our first prayer is about the power of the effectual fervent prayer:

Dear Heavenly Father, your Word says that the effectual, fervent prayer of a righteous man avails much (James 5:16, ULKJV,) that the prayer of a righteous man is powerful and effective (NIV,) and can accomplish much (NASB.) Your Word says that prayers offered by those who have God's approval are effective (ISV,) and exert a mighty influence (WNT.) Very strong is a working supplication of a righteous man (YLT.)

God, I am not righteous by my own righteousness. Your Word teaches that there is none righteous, no, not one (Romans 3:10, ULKJV,) for we are all as an unclean thing, and all our righteousnesses are as filthy rags (Isaiah 64:6, ULKJV.) But in Christ

Jesus am found in Him, not having my own righteousness, which is of the law, but that which is through the faith of Christ, the righteousness which is of God by faith (Philippians 3:9, ULKJV.) I am not righteous in my own righteousness, but I have righteousness by the blood of your Son, Jesus Christ (Romans 5:9, BBE.) It is not by my effort at righteousness but by the righteousness that you grant that I pray the effectual fervent prayers that avail much.[8]

Having therefore, boldness to enter into the holiest by the blood of Jesus (Hebrews 10:19, ULKJV,) I approach you this day in the Name of Jesus (John 14:13 & 16:26.)

In Jesus' Name, Amen

---

[8] Author's exhortation.

The Prayer of Faith

Almighty God,

I come to You in the Name of Jesus, praying the *prayer of faith.*

Your Word says that if I lack wisdom, I should ask of God, that gives to all men liberally, and upbraids not (you don't rebuke me for asking,) and it shall be given unto me. I ask in faith, nothing wavering (not doubting.) For he that wavers is like a wave of the sea driven with the wind and tossed. For let not that man think that he shall receive any thing of the Lord. A double minded man is unstable in all his ways (James 1:5-8, ULKJV.)

This promise does is not only wisdom, but for anything I ask for in prayer. I believe that I have received it, and it will be mine (Mark 11:24, NIV.) Answers to prayer are not limited to spiritual things only, but you also care about my needs (Philippians 4:19) and about my **prosperity** (3 John 2.)

Therefore, I pray these effective, fervent prayers of the righteous in accordance to your Word: My God shall **supply** all my need according to your **riches** in glory by Christ Jesus (Philippians 4:19, ULKJV.) I believe my effective fervent prayers will avail and accomplish much. I believe that you will **supply** my every need according to your **riches** in glory by Christ Jesus.

I also believe that I am your beloved, and that you wish above all things that I may **prosper** and be in health, even as my soul **prospers** (3 John 2, ULKJV.)

I pray with faith because these prayers are powered by your Word. Faith comes by hearing, and hearing by the Word of God (Romans 10:17, ULKJV.) Therefore, I pray these Scripture enriched prayers of faith based upon the very promises of God.

God is not a man, that he should lie, nor a son of man, that he should change his mind. Does he speak and then not act? Does he promise and not fulfill? (Numbers 23:19, NIV.) Indeed, you will act on everything that you have spoken, and fulfill everything that you have promised.

I pray that you will stir faith in me and give me clear understanding and conviction that it is indeed your will for me to **prosper** and be in health, even as my soul **prospers** (3 John 2, ULKJV.)

I ask this, in the Name of my Lord Jesus Christ, Amen and amen…

Prosperity and Success

My Wonderful Lord and Heavenly Father,

You are *El Shaddai* - the Lord God Almighty, your will is **prosperity**. For I am your beloved for whom you wish above all things that I may **prosper** and be in health, even as my soul **prospers** (3 John 2, ULKJV.)

For you know the plans you have for me, plans to **prosper** me and not to harm me, plans to give me hope and a future (Jeremiah 29:11, NIV.) The thoughts and plans that you have for me are thoughts and plans for welfare and peace and not for evil, to give me hope in my final outcome (AMP,) and give me an expected end (ULKJV.)

Lord You promised that if I obey and serve you, I shall spend my days in **prosperity**, and my years in pleasures (Job 36:11,

ULKJV.) My greatest pleasure is to delight myself in you, and you shall give me the desires of my heart (Psalms 37:4, ULKJV.)

You send your angel with me and **prosper** my way (Genesis 24:40, ULKJV.) I keep therefore the words of this covenant, and do them that I may **prosper** in all that I do (Deuteronomy 29:9.)

I delight in the law of the LORD; and in your law do I meditate day and night. And I shall be like a tree planted by the rivers of water, that brings forth fruit in my season; my leaf shall not wither; and whatsoever I do shall **prosper** (Psalms 1:3, ULKJV.) Whatsoever I do! All that I do I accomplish (ABPE.) I succeed in everything I do (GWT.)

I have come unto mount Sion, and unto the city of the living God, the heavenly Jerusalem (Hebrews 12:22, ULKJV,) and I pray for the peace of Jerusalem, and I shall **prosper** (Psalms 122:6, ULKJV.)

As you were with Moses, so you will be with me: you will not fail me, nor forsake me. Therefore, I am strong and of good courage. strong and very courageous, that I may observe to do according to all the law … that I may **prosper** wherever I go. This book of the law shall not depart out of my mouth; but I shall meditate therein day and night, that I may observe to do according to all that is written therein: for then I shall make my way **prosperous** and then I shall have good **success**! (Joshua1:5-8, ULKJV.)

So Lord, I ask of you, let now your ear be attentive to the prayer of your servant … who desires to fear your name: and **prosper**, I pray of you, your servant this day, and grant me mercy (Nehemiah 1:11, ULKJV.)

For You are planting seeds of peace and **prosperity** in my life (Zechariah 8:12, NLT.) That seed is **prosperous**; the vine shall give her fruit, and the ground shall give her **increase**, and the heavens shall give their dew; and you will cause the remnant of this people to possess all these *things* (ULKJV.)

I cleave to the LORD, and depart not from following you … the LORD is with me; and I **prosper** wherever I go forth (2 Kings 18:7, ULKJV.)

I seek my God, I do it with all my heart, and I **prosper** (2 Chronicles 31:21, ULKJV.) As long as I seek the LORD, God makes me to **prosper** (2 Chronicles 26:5, ULKJV.)

I pray and proclaim all of your promises in the most holy and most powerful name of the Lord Jesus Christ, Amen.

With God All Things Are Possible

Oh my God and Heavenly Father,

Your Word says you are the Almighty God (Genesis 17:11, ULKJV.) Therefore, there is nothing impossible with you. With men it is impossible, but not with God: for with God **all things are possible** (Mark 10:27, ULKJV.) Yes, humanly speaking, it is impossible. But not with God. Everything is possible with God (NLT.)

God, **nothing is impossible** with you (Luke 1:37, ULKJV,) yes, **nothing is impossible** with respect to any of your promises (ISV.) Oh Lord, nothing is difficult for you (ABPE.) No word from God shall be void of power (ASV.) No promise from God will be impossible of fulfillment (WNT,) for everything spoken by God is possible (WEB.)

Oh, Lord GOD! Behold, you have made the heaven and the earth by your great power and stretched out arm, and there is **nothing too hard** for you (Jeremiah 32:17, ULKJV.) You said, "Behold, I am the LORD, the God of all flesh: is there any thing too hard for me?" (Jeremiah 32:27, ULKJV.)

No Lord, there is **nothing too hard for** you Lord. Therefore, I rejoice because no matter what I am going through – **nothing is impossible** for God in my life, and *there is* no restraint to the LORD to save by many or by few (1 Samuel 14:6, ULKJV.)

I shall not limit the Holy One of Israel (Psalm 78:41, ULKJV) for **my God can do all things**. You are able to do **exceedingly abundantly** above all that we can ask or think, according to the power that works in us (Ephesians 3:20, ULKJV.) And you are the One Who, by (in consequence of) the [action of your] power that is at work within us, is able to [carry out your purpose and] do **superabundantly**, far over and above all that we [dare] ask or think [infinitely beyond our highest prayers, desires, thoughts, hopes, or dreams] (Ephesians 3:20, AMP.)

Nothing is impossible with you, my Lord.

In Jesus Name, Amen…

The Blessing of the Lord

Heavenly Father,

I thank you for your **blessing** today. For the **blessing** of the LORD, it makes **rich**, and He adds no sorrow with it (Proverbs 10:22, ULKJV.) Your Word teaches that it is the LORD's **blessing** that makes a person **rich**, and hard work adds nothing to it (GWT,) and sorrowful labor add nothing more to it.[9]

I praise you Lord, for **blessed** is the man who fears the Lord, who finds great delight in his commands. My children will be mighty in the land; the generation of the upright will be **blessed**. **Wealth** and **riches** are in my house, and my righteousness endures forever. Even in darkness light dawns for the upright, for the gracious and compassionate and righteous man. Good will come to

[9] Direct translation from the old Afrikaans translation: "Die seën van die Here- dit maak ryk, en moeitevolle arbeid voeg daar niks by nie".

me for I am generous and lend freely, and I conduct my affairs with justice (prudently, sensibly, economically, wisely[10].) Surely I will never be shaken; a righteous man will be remembered forever. I will have no fear of bad news; my heart is steadfast, trusting in the Lord. My heart is secure; I will have no fear; in the end I will look in triumph on my foes. I have scattered abroad my gifts to the poor, my righteousness endures forever and my horn (authority, dignity and influence[11]) will be lifted high in honor! (Psalm 112:1-9, NIV.)

Father God, you will bless me in such a way that I am not only **blessed**, but I will **be a blessing** (Genesis 12:2, ULKJV.) My cup is not only filled – it runs over (Psalms 23:5, ULKJV.) From the overflow of your **blessings**, I become a **blessing** by **blessing** others.[12]

I pray and proclaim all of your promises in the most holy and most powerful name of the Lord Jesus Christ, Amen.

---

[10] Barnes' Notes on the Bible, Albert Barnes 1884, Baker Books.
[11] Author's explanation on the symbolic meaning of *horn*.
[12] Author's exhortation based on these Scriptures.

El Shaddai

Oh Almighty God and my Heavenly Father,

Your nature is revealed in your Names. You changed Abram's name to *Abraham* - the father of many nations (Genesis 17:5, ULKJV.) You changed Jacob's (the coward or deceiver) to *Israel* (Genesis 32:27-28, ULKJV) (a prince and conqueror with God.[13])

So too I take special note of how you reveal yourself in the Scriptures by your Names.

Your Word says you are *El Shaddai* – the Almighty God (Genesis 17:1, ULKJV,) the Burly, Powerful and Impregnable One[14] - the Strong and Breasted One, the Strong-Nourisher, Strength-

---

[13] Meaning of the Hebrew word *Israel.*

[14] Strong's Hebrew word # 7706/7703: *Shaddai.*

Giver, Satisfier, All-Bountiful, the Supplier of the needs of your people. [15]

The old song says[16],

"You are more than enough, more than enough. You are El Shaddai, the God of Plenty. The All Sufficient One, God Almighty, Jesus, you're more than enough."

This day I confirm that I stand in covenant with the same *El Shaddai* that Abraham worshiped, for the **blessing** of Abraham has come upon me (Galatians 3:14.)

El Shaddai, you are burly (large and strong.) You are noble, handsome and very excellent. El Shaddai, you are Powerful. You are **all powerful** because you are the **Almighty God**. You have the highest ability to act or affect strongly, with unlimited vigor, force and strength. You are El Shaddai, the Impregnable, not capable of being captured or be entered by force. You are unshakable, unyielding and firm, and you are on *my* side.[17]

With a God like you by my side, who can be against me? (Romans 8:31, ULKJV.) With a God like you by my side, **nothing is impossible** (Luke 1:37, ULKJV.) With men it is impossible, but not with God: for with God **all things are possible** (Mark 10:2, ULKJV.)

[15] Dake's Annotated Reference Bible Page 14, Column 1, note M
[16] From the song He's more than enough by David Ingles
[17] Excerpts from Strong's Hebrew and Webster's dictionary.

If I can believe, **all things are possible** to me that believes (Mark 9:23, ULKJV.)

I pray and proclaim all of your promises in the most holy and most powerful name of the Lord Jesus Christ, Amen.

Jehovah Jireh

Dear God,

Your Word teaches that you are *Jehovah Jireh*[18] - the **LORD my Provider** (Genesis 22:14, ULKJV.) You are *the Lord Who sees and foresees*[19]. You know what I will need tomorrow, because you see and foresee. You know today what I need tomorrow, and you knew yesterday what I needed today.

The God Who knew what I needed is also the God who **provided** for me in advance. My Father knows that I have need of these things (Matthew 6:32, ULKJV.) You are Jehovah Jireh, the **Lord my Provider**.

---

[18] God's Name was revealed as the Tetragrammatons YHWH in the Old Testament, which has been pronounced as "Yahweh" or "Jehovah". We may use either pronunciation, for it has the same meaning – the LORD, as it has been translated in most Bible translations.

[19] Meaning of the Hebrew *Yireh* or *Jireh.*

My God shall **supply** in all my needs according to your **riches** in glory by Christ Jesus (Philippians 4:19, ULKJV.) The young lions do lack and suffer hunger, but I seek the LORD and therefore **I do not want or lack any good thing** (Psalms 34:10, ULKJV,) because Jehovah Jireh is the **Lord my Provider**.

I shall not lack any good *thing*, promise, speech, word[20] or tangible object.[21] I shall not lack any beautiful, best or **bountiful** thing. In my life there is no lack of cheerful things, fine things, gracious, joyful or loving things. I **abound** with merry things and pleasant things - things associated with **prosperity**, sweet things and things associated with **wealth**.[22]

You are Jehovah Jireh, the **Lord my Provider**, and in the mount of the LORD it shall be seen (Genesis 22:14, ULKJV.) The mount of the LORD is *Mount Calvary*, in the Hebrew tongue *Golgotha* (John 19:17, ULKJV.) This is where you died on the Cross for me. This is where Abraham rejoiced to see your day, and he saw it and was glad (John 8:56, Genesis 22:4, ULKJV.)

It is in your atoning death on the Mount of the Lord that I receive every benefit as a child of God, for it is in the mount of the LORD that it shall be seen – from where your **provision** comes. It's

[20] Strong's Hebrew word # 562 *omer*.
[21] Webster's.
[22] Strong's Hebrew word # 2896 *towb*.

where Jesus died for me and made me eligible for every **blessing** I can receive from God. It is on the cross that you delivered me from the curse and brought upon me the **blessings** (Galatians 3:13-14, ULKJV.) Thanks be to God who has **blessed** me with all spiritual **blessings** in heavenly places in Christ Jesus (Ephesians 1:3, ULKJV.)

You are indeed *Jehovah Jireh* – my **Provider**. You are *Jehovah Rohi* – the LORD my Shepherd. And because the LORD is my Shepherd and I shall not want (Psalms 23:1, ULKJV!)

I pray and proclaim all the things in the mighty Name of Jesus, Amen.

The Blessing of Abraham

Dear Almighty God and my Heavenly Father,

You blessed Abraham and the nation of Israel, and as spiritual Israel those **blessings** are mine (Genesis 12:1-3; 16:1-6; 17:1-2; Deuteronomy 28:1-14; Galatians 6:16; 1 Corinthians 1:20, Galatians 3:13-14.) The **blessings** of Abraham are mine, and I pray and proclaim that every one of them will be manifested in my life (Galatians 3:13-14, ULKJV.) All the promises of God are 'yes' and 'amen' in Christ Jesus (1 Corinthians 1:20, ULKJV.)

Christ has redeemed us from the curse of the law, being made a curse for us: for it is written, Cursed is every one that hangs on a tree: that the **blessing** of Abraham might come on the Gentiles through Jesus Christ; that we might receive the promise of the Spirit through faith (Galatians 3:13-14, ULKJV.)

Today I refuse the curse of the law as outlined in Deuteronomy 28. I shall not be cursed in the city, nor cursed in the field. Neither are my basket and store cursed. Neither the fruit of my body, land, the **increase** of my herd and the flocks of my sheep. I am not cursed when I come in nor cursed when I go out. I refuse the curse of vexation, rebuke, destruction, pestilence, consumption, fever, inflammation, extreme burning, the sword, blasting, mildew and every other curse, because Jesus, when you hung and died on the cross you took removed the curse (Deuteronomy 28:15-29, Galatians 3:13.)

Rather, I receive the **blessings**! The LORD sets me high above all the nations of the earth and all these **blessings** shall come on me and overtake me because I hearken unto the voice of the LORD my God (Deuteronomy 28:1-2,) and because Jesus, you died on the cross that the **blessings** of Abraham would come upon me (Galatians 3:12-14.) Blessed shall I be in the city and **blessed** shall I be in the field. Blessed shall be the fruit of my body and the fruit of my ground. Blessed shall be the fruit of my cattle, the **increase** of my herd, and the flocks of my sheep. Blessed shall be my basket and my store. Blessed shall I be when I come in and **blessed** shall I be when I go out.

The LORD shall cause my enemies that rise up against me to be smitten before my face: they shall come out against me one way, and flee before me seven ways. The LORD shall command the **blessing** upon me in my storehouses, and in all that I set my hand unto; and You shall bless me in the land which the LORD my God gives to me.

The LORD shall establish me holy unto yourself, as You have sworn unto me, if I keep the commandments of the LORD my God and walk in Your ways. And all the people of the earth shall see that I am called by the Name of the LORD and they shall respect me greatly.

And the LORD shall make me **plenteous** in goods, in the fruit of my body, and in the fruit of my cattle, and in the fruit of my ground, in the land which the LORD has promised me. You give unto me your good treasure, the heaven to give rain unto my land in his season, and to bless all the work of my hand.

I shall lend unto many and I shall not borrow. LORD, you make me the head, and not the tail; and I shall be above only, and not beneath; for I hearken unto your commandments... (Deuteronomy 28:1-14, ULKJV.)

This is the **blessing** of the law and the **blessing** of Abraham and Israel that you promise me. All the promises of God are 'yes' and 'amen' in Christ Jesus. Anything on the contrary I shall resist. I resist it today, in the Name of Jesus.

I pray and proclaim all of your promises in the mighty and beautiful name of Jesus, Amen.

Authority over the spirit of Poverty

My Dear Heavenly Father and Lord God Almighty,

Today I choose to believe your Word, rather than the unbiblical traditions of men. For there are those who nullify and make the Word of God of none effect by the traditions of men, being passed down from the blind leading the blind, from generation to generation (Mark 7:13, Luke 6:39, ULKJV.)

Today I refuse to blindly follow the unbiblical traditions of men that have tried to rob from me your promises of **prosperity** as they are revealed in your Word. I resist teachings that have a form of godliness, but deny the power thereof. From such I turn away (2 Timothy 3:5, ULKJV.)

I renounce wolfish teaching in sheep's clothing. False teaching and false prophets come in sheep's clothing, but inwardly they are ravening wolves (Matthew 7:15, ULKJV.) You don't promise poverty and lack, rather you promise **prosperity** and **abundance**.

For it is not you, but it is the thief that comes not but to steal, kill and destroy (John 10:10, ULKJV.) Rather, you came that I may have life and have it more **abundantly** (John 10:10, ULKJV.)

It is not you who impoverished Israel, for Israel was greatly impoverished because of the Midianites (Judges 6:6, ULKJV.) When they called on the LORD, you delivered them from their poverty, and I call upon you today.

Whoever shall call upon the Name of the Lord shall be saved (Romans 10:13, ULKJV.) If I shall be saved from sin if I call upon your Name for salvation, you will also save me from poverty and lack as I call upon your Name for **prosperity** and **abundance** (Judges 6:6, ULKJV.)

Israel wandered in the wilderness in a desert way; they found no city of habitation. Hungry and thirsty, their soul fainted in them. Then they cried unto Jehovah in their trouble, and he delivered them out of their distresses (Psalms 107:4-6, ASV.) I call upon you today and you deliver me from my distresses.

Because I stand in a **giving** and receiving relationship with you by my tithe and offering, I also know that you rebuke the devourer for my sake (Malachi 3:11, ULKJV.) The *devourer* is the devil, and the spirit of poverty that eats and burns up my resources.[23] It is the enemy - the spirit of poverty that devours resources. It is he that eats up hungrily, greedily and voraciously, consumes and destroys with a devastating force.[24]

The devourer is a worker of iniquity that eat up your people as if they eat bread (Psalms 53:4, ULKJV.) Therefore, I am sober and vigilant; because my adversary the devil, as a roaring lion, walks about, seeking whom he may devour (1 Peter 5:8, ULKJV.) I am God's property and I refuse to allow the spirit of poverty eat me as if I'm bread (Psalms 53:4, ULKJV.) I soberly and with great vigilance recognize that it is the devil who is the devourer, and that my God shall rebuke the devourer for my sake (Malachi 3:11, ULKJV.)

It is the LORD that rebukes the devourer for my sake (Malachi 3:11, ULKJV.) The LORD chides, corrupts, rebukes and reproves the devourer for my sake.[25] You chide and scold the devourer on my behalf, oh God. You corrupt him and change him from a sound condition to an unsound one. You reprove, refute and disprove him.[26]

The devourer will regret his attacks on me. For we wrestle not against flesh and blood, but against principalities, against

---

[23] Strong's Hebrew word # 398: *akal.*
[24] Webster's for *devour.*
[25] Strong's Hebrew word # 1605 *gaar.*
[26] Webster's.

powers, against the rulers of the darkness of this world, against spiritual wickedness in high places (Ephesians 6:12, ULKJV.)

If the princes of this world (the principalities and dark spirit beings)[27] knew the wisdom of God, they would not have crucified the Lord of Glory (1 Corinthians 2:8, ULKJV,)[28] for it was on the cross that Jesus wrought for us the victory. In the same way, if the devourer had known the wisdom of God, he would not have attacked me financially. his attacks have made me more determined to believe the Word of God and taste the promises of God.[29]

My faith has gone through a trial and is much more precious than of gold that perishes. Though it be tried with fire, it will be found unto praise and honor and glory at the appearing of Jesus Christ (1 Peter 1:7, ULKJV.)[30] The LORD turns my captivity and gives me at least[31] twice as much as I had before (Job 42:10, ULKJV.) The LORD restores my fortunes and **increases** all I have at least twofold (NASB.)

The devourer, the thief, yes the spirit of poverty shall restore sevenfold; he shall give all the substance of his house (Proverbs

[27] Explanation by author who is referred to as *princes* - Ephesians 6:12.
[28] This is one of the greatest revelations in the Word of God: Satan and his princes were completely oblivious that it would be in the very death and resurrection of Christ that salvation and all New Testament benefits would come to mankind.
[29] Author's exhortation.
[30] This appearing of Christ includes his ultimate second coming, but it may also be applied to his coming with our provision.
[31] Author's exhortation: Not limited to only twice as much (Ephesians 3:20.)

6:31, ULKJV.) My enemy has come up against me in one way but flees from me seven ways (Deuteronomy 28:7, ULKJV.)

I bind the strongman of poverty and spoil his house (Mark 3:26, ULKJV.) Whatsoever I bind on earth shall be bound in heaven, and whatsoever I loose on earth shall be loosed in heaven (Deuteronomy 18:18, ULKJV.) I bind the spirit of poverty and lack, and I release the **abundance** of God into my life.

I resist the devil steadfast in the faith and shall flee from me (1 Peter 1:9; James 4:7, ULKJV.) The Lord rebukes the devourer for my sake (Malachi 3:11, ULKJV.)

Thank you God that you rebuke the spirit of poverty in my life and bless me with your abundance and provision!

I pray and proclaim all these things in the mighty Name of Jesus, Amen.

Abundant Life

Dear Heavenly Father and Almighty God,

I come to you in the Name of Jesus Christ. I thank you for my salvation and for every gift you have so wonderfully bestowed upon my life, for every good gift and every perfect gift is from above, and comes down from the Father of lights, with whom is no variableness, neither shadow of turning (James 1:17, ULKJV.)

I thank you for the gift of **abundant life**. The thief comes not, but for to steal, and to kill, and to destroy, but you have come that I may have life, and that I may have it more **abundantly** (John 10:10, ULKJV.) You are a **God of abundance**. Your nature is **abundance**. When you created the universe, you didn't create barely enough.[32] You created innumerable planets, stars and outer space, and you did it for man. When I consider your heavens, the

[32] Author's Exhortation based on Psalms 8:3-5.

work of your fingers, the moon and the stars, which you have ordained; What is man, that you are mindful of him? and the son of man, that you visit him? For you have made him a little lower than the angels, and hast crowned him with glory and honor (Psalms 8:3-5, ULKJV.)

Lord, you are a **God of abundance**, and Jesus, you came that I may have life more **abundantly**. You came that I may have a life beyond measure, a life **superabundant** in quantity and superior in quality, an excessive life which is exceeding **abundantly** above all that I can ask or think[33] (Ephesians 3:20, ULKJV.) You are a **God of abundance**.

I am your servant, your handmaid, and you have pleasure in my **prosperity** (Psalms 35:27, ULKJV.) You grant me **abundant prosperity** (Deuteronomy 28:11, NIV,) and bless me with **abundant provisions** (Psalms 132:15, NIV.) The profit of the wicked and her earnings will be set apart for the Lord; they will not be stored up or hoarded. Her profits will go to those who live before the Lord, for **abundant food and fine clothes**. I live before the Lord, and I shall have **abundant food and fine clothes**. (Isaiah 23:18, NIV.)

I will bring you renown, joy, praise and honor before all nations on earth that hear of all the good things you have done for

---

[33] Strong's Greek word # 4053: *perissos.*

me; and they will be in awe and will tremble at the **abundant prosperity** and peace you have **provided** for me (Jeremiah 33:9, NIV.)

You are a **God of abundance**, with a great **supply**, more than sufficient quantity, **wealth**, very **plentiful**, more than sufficient and ample; and you wish for your people to be **well supplied** and **rich**.[34] you **supply beyond measure**, and you bless me with **life that is superabundant in quantity and superior in quality**.

For you can do **exceeding, abundantly above** all that we ask or think (Ephesians 3:20, ULKJV.) Now to Him Who, by (in consequence of) the [action of his] power that is at work within us, is able to [carry out his purpose and] do **superabundantly**, far over and above all that we [dare] ask or think [infinitely beyond our highest prayers, desires, thoughts, hopes, or dreams] – to Him be glory in the church and in Christ Jesus throughout all generations forever and ever (Ephesians 3:20, AMP.)

Today I acknowledge that **abundance** is the exact opposite of scarcity and lack. You do not will for your people to suffer hunger, scarcity and lack. Your will is **abundance**.[35] The young

---

[34] Webster's: Latin word *abundantia*. The line following also continues the meaning of the word *abundance*.

[35] Author's exhortation based on Psalm 34:1.

lions do lack, and suffer hunger: but they that seek the LORD shall not want any good thing (Psalms 34:1, ULKJV.)

Just as when Israel captured fortified cities and fertile land; I too take possession of houses filled with all kinds of good things, wells already dug, vineyards, olive groves and fruit trees in **abundance**. They ate to the full and were **well-nourished**; they **reveled in your great goodness** (Nehemiah 9:25, NIV.)

I will see and be radiant, and my heart will thrill and rejoice; because the **abundance** of the sea will be turned to me, the **wealth** of the nations will come to me (Isaiah 60:5, ULKJV.) I am spiritual Israel, the Israel of God (Galatians 6:16, ULKJV.) I have come unto mount Zion, and unto the city of the living God, the heavenly Jerusalem, and to an innumerable company of angels (Hebrews 12:22, ULKJV.) All the **blessings** of Abraham are mine (Galatians 3:14, ULKJV,) and all the promises of God are 'yes' and 'amen' in Christ Jesus (2 Corinthians 1:20, ULKJV.) Therefore, as spiritual Israel – the Israel of God, I claim those promises as mine. You **abundantly** bless Zion's **provision**: you satisfy her poor with bread (Psalms 132:15, ULKJV.)

There is no man that has left house, or brethren, or sisters, or father, or mother, or wife, or children, or lands, for your sake, and the gospel's, but shall receive **a hundredfold** now in this time, houses, and brethren, and sisters, and mothers, and children, and lands, with persecutions; and in the world to come eternal life (Mark 10:29-30, ULKJV.)

You give me of heaven's dew and of earth's **richness**—an **abundance** of grain and new wine (Genesis 27:28, NIV.) You crown this year with your **bounty**, and my carts overflow with **abundance** (Psalms 65:11, NIV.) I eat the bread of angels: you send me **provisions** in **abundance** (Psalms 78:25, DRB.) I bring my tithes to the storehouse and I bring my offerings to the LORD that there may be **provision** in your house, and you open the windows of heaven and pour me out a **blessing** that there shall not be room enough to receive it (Malachi 3:10, ULKJV), you pour me out a **blessing** even to **abundance** (Malachi 3:10, DRB.)

I have all, and **abound**: I am full (Philippians 4:18, ULKJV.) I have received everything in full and have **abundance**; I am amply supplied (NIV & NASB.) My God shall **supply** in all my need according to his **riches** in glory by Christ Jesus (Philippians 4:19, ULKJV.)

I honor you, oh LORD with my substance, and with the first fruits of all my **increase**: So shall my barns be filled with **plenty** (and **abundance**, DRB), and my presses shall burst out with new wine (Proverbs 3:9-10, ULKJV.)

I work my land, and shall have an **abundance** of food (Proverbs 28:19, NIV.) In much work there shall be **abundance**

(Proverbs 14:23, DRB.) I shall enjoy **abundance** and be full of the **blessing** of the LORD (Deuteronomy 33:23, DRB.) I will not be ashamed in the time of evil, and in the days of famine I will have **abundance** (Psalms 37:19, NASB.)

Today oh Lord, I decide to think in terms of **abundance**, pray in terms of **abundance** and believe in terms of **abundance** and **increase**, multiplied by the myriads, by the ten thousands and by the millions.[36]

In Jesus Name, I refuse to let poverty thinking and unbiblical traditions of men rob me from the **abundance** that you intend for me.

In Jesus' Name, Amen.

[36] Strong's Hebrew word # 7231 *rabah* & # 7233 *rebabah* and Webster's definition of *myriad.*

Royal Abundance

Almighty God,

You washed us from our sins in your his blood we have been made kings and priests unto God and his Father (Acts 20:28, Revelation 1:6, ULKJV.) You will satisfy your priests with **abundance**, and your people will be filled with your **bounty** (Jeremiah 31:14, ULKJV.) My **abundance** will **supply** for the want of my brothers and sisters in the Lord, and vice versa (2 Corinthians 8:14, ULKJV.)

Jesus Christ made me a king and priest unto God (Revelation 1:6, ULKJV.)

As with King David, my **abundance** also makes **provision** for the temple of God and the work of the Lord (1 Chronicles 22:3, 14, ULKJV.) For I too am a king and priest unto God.

As with King Solomon, I too make silver as common as stones, and cedar trees as sycamore trees in **abundance** (2 Chronicles 9:27, ULKJV.) For I too am a king.

As with King Jehoshaphat, I also have **riches** and honor in **abundance** (2 Chronicles 17:5, ULKJV.) The **abundance** of the seas is mine, and so is the treasures hid in the sand (Deuteronomy 33:19, ULKJV.) For I have been made a king.

As a King and a priest unto God (Revelation 1:6, ULKJV,) I have **abundance** like King Hezekiah had. And Hezekiah had exceeding much **riches** and honor: and he made himself treasuries for silver, and for gold, and for precious stones, and for spices, and for shields, and for all manner of pleasant jewels; Storehouses also for the **increase** of corn, and wine, and oil; and stalls for all manner of beasts, and cotes for flocks. Moreover, he **provided** him cities and possessions of flocks and herds in **abundance**: for God had given him substance very much (2 Chronicles 31:27-29.) If God **blessed** Hezekiah in the Old Covenant like this, how much the more will my God bless me in the New Covenant, which is established on even better promises (Hebrews 8:6, ULKJV.) Both the Old and New Testament promises are mine. All the promises of God are 'yes' and 'amen' in Christ Jesus (2 Corinthians 1:20, ULKJV.) [37]

---

[37] Though luxuries are not intrinsically wrong, the author is not implying that we are to indulge in luxury, but that we may indeed believe God for abundance. The reader is also exhorted that the

By the blood of Jesus, I am a priest and a king (Revelation 1:5-6, ULKJV.) Because I am a king, I aspire to be a king and give like a king, in the *manner of* **abundance** (1 Kings 10:10, ULKJV.) I enter into the rhythm of **giving** and receiving (Luke 6:38,) and I shall have *more* **abundance** (Matthew 13:12.) The **wealth** of the heathen is mine—gold, silver, and apparel, *in great* **abundance** (Zechariah 14:14, ULKJV.)

I bring in **abundance** the first fruits of corn, wine, and oil, and honey, and of all the **increase** of the field; and the tithe of all things I bring in **abundantly**, as an offering unto my God (2 Chronicles 31:5, ULKJV.)

I pray and proclaim all of your promises in the most holy and most powerful name of the Lord Jesus Christ, Amen.

spiritual riches of Christ should be pursued more than the temporal things of this world that have no eternal value.

No need to Fret or Covet

Father, when I experience trying financial times, I thank you that it gives me the opportunity to fight and overcome lack with the power of faith for your **abundant provision**, and to remind myself that my love and affection is on you, not in my possessions. The brother in humble circumstances ought to take pride in his high position. But the one who is **rich** should take pride in his low position, because he will pass away like a wild flower. For the sun rises with scorching heat and withers the plant; its blossom falls and its beauty is destroyed. In the same way, the **rich** man will fade away even while he goes about his business (James 1:9-11, ULKJV.)

He that loveth silver shall not be satisfied with silver; nor he that loveth **abundance** with **increase** (Ecclesiastes 5:10, ULKJV.) My life does not revolve around the **abundance** of things I possess (Luke 12:15, ULKJV.)

I shall not bow before Mammon, for no man can serve both God and Mammon (Matthew 6:24, ULKJV.) For the love of money is the root of all evil: which while some coveted after, they have erred from the faith, and pierced themselves through with many sorrows (1 Timothy 6:10, ULKJV.) Thank you God that I need not bow before Mammon, for my God Himself **provide**s for me.[38]

I need not be high-minded, nor trust in uncertain **riches**, but in the living God, who gives to me **richly** all things to enjoy (1 Timothy 6:17, ULKJV.) All the **blessings**, whether they be spiritual or material are mine to enjoy, because my God is a **God of abundance**.[39]

I shall not be as the man that made not God his strength; but trusted in the **abundance** of his **riches**, and strengthened himself in his wickedness. But I am like a green olive tree in the house of God. (Psalms 53:7-8, ULKJV.) Surely goodness and mercy shall follow me all the days of my life, and I will dwell in the house of the Lord forever (Psalms 23:6, ULKJV.)

I serve the LORD my God with joyfulness, and with gladness of heart, for the **abundance** of all things; or else I will serve my enemies (Deuteronomy 28:47, ULKJV.)

---

[38] Author's exhortation.
[39] Author's exhortation based on 1 Timothy 6:17.

you are the giver of **abundance**. But you are a jealous God, and will not that I share my love with any other god but you, including mammon and covetousness, which is idolatry (Exodus 34:14, Matthew 6:24, Colossians 3:5, ULKJV.)

I will be careful and vigilant to guard against those false prophets also among the people, even as there shall be false teachers among us, who privily shall bring in damnable heresies, even denying the Lord that bought them, and bring upon themselves swift destruction. And many shall follow their pernicious ways; by reason of whom the way of truth shall be evil spoken of. And through covetousness shall they with feigned words make merchandise of us: whose judgment now of a long time lingers not, and their damnation slumbers not (2 Peter 2:1-3, ULKJV.)

As is proper for saints, I will not let sexual sin, impurity of any kind, or greed even be mentioned among us (Ephesians 5:3, NIV.) I refuse to be filled with all unrighteousness, fornication, wickedness and covetousness (Romans 1:29, ULKJV.) And because I hate covetousness, I shall prolong my days (Proverbs 28:16, ULKJV.)

The proof that I have overcome greed and covetousness is the fact that I am a giver.[40] A man may give freely, and still his

---

[40] Exhortation by author. It makes good sense that the act of giving our resources is not only proof of victory over covetousness, but also a weapon to fight it with.

wealth will be **increase**d; and another may keep back more than is right, but only comes to be in need (Proverbs 11:24, BBE,) and it tends to poverty (ULKJV.) I serve the God of **abundant provision**, and therefore I need not serve mammon (Matthew 6:24, ULKJV.)

I don't seek to build my own kingdom, but rather seek God's kingdom first, and all these things shall be added unto me (Matthew 6:33, ULKJV.) I seek God's kingdom first. I seek, go about, and desire your kingdom first.[41] I seek, bend my efforts toward, aim at and pursue your kingdom.[42] I wish, long for, crave and covet your kingdom, with a sense of intense longing, intensity and ardor.[43]

Because I seek and covet your kingdom, and because my priorities are focused on your kingdom first, I do not need to covet the things of this world. Rather, they are freely given to me to enjoy (1 Timothy 6:17, ULKJV) and all these things are added unto me (Matthew 6:33, ULKJV.)

The love of money is the root of all evil (1 Timothy 6:10, ULKJV,) and therefore I refuse to love money or put my affections on it. Rather, I serve, worship and set my affections on God and your kingdom, and as a result, both spiritual and material possessions will be added unto me. I shall not covet (Exodus 20:17, ULKJV,) because

---

[41] Strong's Greek word # 2212: *zeteo.*
[42] Webster's for *seek.*
[43] Webster's for *desire*.

my God **supplies** in all my needs (Philippians 4:19, ULKJV.) When I give, I give from the **bounty** God gave me, and expect his **bountiful supply**, and shall not allow covetousness to influence or minimize my **giving** into the kingdom of God (2 Corinthians 9:5.) My manner of life is without covetousness; and I am content with such things as I have: for you have said, I will never leave you, nor forsake you. (Hebrews 13:5, ULKJV.) I am content, I have enough and I am satisfied with God's **abundant provision**[44]. *You* **provide** me with all I need. I have food and raiment to the point of contentment, enough and satisfaction (1 Timothy 6:8.)

I know what it is to be in need, and I know what it is to have **plenty**. I have learned the secret of being content (*having enough and be satisfied*) in any and every situation, whether well fed or hungry, whether living in **plenty** or in want, and I can do all things through Christ who strengthens me (Philippians 4:12-13, NIV/ULKJV.)

There is no need for covetousness in my life, for my God is my **provider**. In Jesus' Name I pray, Amen.

---

[44] Strong's Greek words # 714: *arkeo* and # 713 *arketos*.

Sowing and Reaping

Oh God Almighty,

You will not violate the principles of **giving** and receiving, of sowing and reaping, for while the earth remains, seedtime and harvest, and cold and heat, and summer and winter, and day and night shall not cease (Genesis 8:22, ULKJV.)

you said that whatsoever a man sows, he shall also reap (Galatians 6:7, ULKJV.) Therefore, I will not be weary in well doing: for in due season I shall reap, if I faint not (Galatians 6:9, ULKJV.)

And you are not mocked: For whatsoever a man sows, that shall he also reap (Galatians 6:7, ULKJV.) Thank you God that you will not be mocked in the realm of sowing and reaping, **giving** and receiving. If I sow and I reap not, you will be mocked. But you will not be mocked. You will ensure that the principles of **giving** and receiving, sowing and reaping are indeed upheld, for your Word is your honor.[45]

Even in famine (Genesis 26:1) I sow in the land, and I receive in the same year a hundredfold: and the LORD blesses me. And I wax great, and go forward, and grow until I became very great: For I have possession of flocks, and possession of herds, and great store of servants: and the Philistines shall envy me (Genesis 26:12-14, ULKJV.) It is by your **blessing** that the roles shall be reversed, for the Philistines shall be jealous of me (Genesis 26:14, GWT.)

I shall also sow liberally, for he that sows sparingly shall reap also sparingly; and he that sows **bountifully** shall reap also **bountifully** (2 Corinthians 9:6, ULKJV.) I plant generously and shall have a generous crop (NLT.) For the farmer who plants a few seeds will have a very small harvest. But the farmer who plants because he has received God's **blessings** will receive a harvest of God's **blessings** in return (GWT.)

I scatter everywhere and give to the poor; my righteousness lasts forever (2 Corinthians 9:9, ULKJV.) I believe your Word, for you have said that he that ministers seed to the sower both ministers bread for my food, and **multiply** my seed sown, and **increase** the

---

[45] Exhortation by the author based on Galatians 6:7-9. The apostle Paul taught that God will not be mocked in not honoring his principle of sowing and reaping.

fruits of my righteousness (2 Corinthians 9:10, ULKJV.) He who **supplies** seed to the sower and bread for food will **supply** and **multiply** my seed for sowing and **increase** the harvest of my righteousness (NASB.)

I am enriched in every thing to all **bountifulness**, which causes through me thanks**giving** to God (2 Corinthians 9:11, ULKJV.) I will be enriched in every way to be generous in every way, which through me will produce thanks**giving** to God (ESV.) In every way I will grow **richer** and become even more generous, and this will cause others to give thanks to God because of me (ISV.)

Thank you God, for the principle of sowing and reaping, and that you will uphold this principle that you have set.

I pray and proclaim your promises in the mighty and holy name of Jesus, Amen.

Give and It shall be Given

Dear Lord God,

I remember the words of the Lord Jesus, how he said, It is more **blessed** [makes one happier and more to be envied,] (AMP) to give than to receive (Acts 20:35, ULKJV.)

Therefore, I give, and it shall be given unto me; good measure, pressed down, and shaken together, and running over, shall men give into my bosom. For with the same measure that I mete withal it shall be measured to me again (Luke 6:38, ULKJV.)

I give, and I will receive. My gift will return to me in full - pressed down, shaken together to make room for more, running over, and poured into my lap. The amount I give will determine the amount I get back (NLT.)

I give, and I will receive. A large quantity, pressed together, shaken down, and running over will be put into my pocket. The standards I use for others will be applied to me (GWT.)

I give, and [gifts] will be given to me; good measure, pressed down, shaken together, and running over, will they pour into [the pouch formed by] the bosom [of my robe and used as a bag]. For with the measure I deal out [with the measure I use when I confer benefits on others], it will be measured back to me (AMP.)

Father, you are a giver yourself, for you gave your Son, that whosoever believes on Him should not perish but have eternal life (John 3:16, ULKJV.) Thanks be to God for your unspeakable gift (2 Corinthians 9:15, ULKJV), your indescribable gift (NIV), a gift too wonderful for words (NLT) – Jesus, your Son!

By your grace and power oh God, I am a giver. Because I am a giver and because I am in covenant with you, I give with cheerfulness.

I give what I have decided in my heart to give, not reluctantly or under compulsion (not grudgingly, or of necessity, ULKJV,) for God loves a cheerful giver (2 Corinthians 9:7, NIV.)

I [give] as I have made up my own mind and purposed in my heart, not reluctantly or sorrowfully or under compulsion, for God loves (You take pleasure in, you prize above other things, and you are unwilling to abandon or to do without) a cheerful (joyous, "prompt to do it") giver [whose heart is in his **giving**] (AMP.)

God I know you love the whole world (John 3:16,) but because you make special mention of cheerful givers, boisterously merry givers,[46] you reveal that your love for cheerful givers is unique. In harmony with the rest of your Word I know that you will bless me in return for my **giving**.[47]

I pray and proclaim all of your promises in the most holy and most powerful name of the Lord Jesus Christ, Amen.

---

[46] The Greek word for *cheerful* here is *hilaron*, from which we get our English word *hilarious*. Hilarious mean *boisterously merry*.

[47] Author's exhortation.

Honor the Lord with My Substance

My Lord and my God,

I honor the LORD with my substance, and with the first fruits of all my **increase** (Proverbs 3:9, ULKJV,) yes I honor the LORD with my **wealth** and with the **best part** of everything I produce (NLT) and **best part** of all my income (GWT.) So shall my barns be filled with **plenty**, and my presses shall burst out with new wine (Proverbs 3:10, ULKJV.)

I bring my tithes into the storehouse, that there may be meat in your house, and I prove you now herewith, Oh LORD of hosts, if you will not open me the windows of heaven, and pour me out a **blessing**, that there shall not be room enough to receive it (Malachi 3:10, ULKJV.) Indeed, I bring one-tenth of my income into the storehouse so that there may be food in your house. I test you in this way, Oh LORD of Armies and see if you won't open the windows of heaven for me and **flood me with blessings** (GWT,) until it overflows (NASB) and there is **no more need** (ESV.)[48]

Therefore, I shall partner with the Gospel in accordance with the principles of **giving** and receiving. And as I support the Gospel, **fruit will abound to my account**. My **giving** to the work of the Lord is a sweet smell, a sacrifice acceptable, well-pleasing to God. And my God shall **supply** all my need according to his **riches** in glory by Christ Jesus (Philippians 4:15-18, ULKJV.)[49]

I pray and proclaim all of your promises in the most holy and most powerful name of the Lord Jesus Christ, Amen.

---

[48] The principle of tithing in the Old Testament is affirmed by Jesus in the New Testament: "Woe unto you, scribes and Pharisees, hypocrites! for you all pay tithe of mint and anise and cummin, and have omitted the weightier *matters* of the law, judgment, mercy, and faith: these ought you all to have done, and not to leave the other undone" (Matthew 23:23, ULKJV.) Still tithing should not be done not grudgingly, or of necessity: for God loveth a cheerful giver (2 Corinthians 9:7, ULKJV) whose heart is in his giving (AMP.)

[49] This paragraph is purposely repeated in the prayer "I advance God's kingdom by what God blessed me with," for giving has to do with supporting the spreading of the Gospel.

Advance the Kingdom with my Wealth

Oh my Lord God and Heavenly Father,

You are the King of kings and Lord of lords (Revelation 19:6, ULKJV.) Today I am reminded of the bigger picture – that you are setting up your kingdom, and that your dealings with me are intimately tied to your kingdom, the advancement of it, the spreading of the Gospel, your desire to fill the earth with your glory and to establish your covenant.[50]

Therefore, I seek first the kingdom of God and all these things shall be added unto me (Matthew 6:33, ULKJV.) I make your kingdom and righteousness my chief aim, and then these things shall all be given me in addition (WNT.) I am first concerned about your kingdom and what has your approval. Then all these things will be

[50] Author's exhortation based on the Scriptures used in the prayer in this chapter.

provided for me (GWT.) I seek the kingdom of God above all else, and live righteously, and you will give me everything I need (NLT.)

As truly as you live, all the earth shall be filled with the glory of the LORD (Numbers 14:21, ULKJV.) This is your greater plan, your grand intent – that the earth shall be filled with the glory of the Lord. And I acknowledge today that your **blessings** on me is to further this cause.

I shout for joy and I am glad for I favor your righteous cause. I say continually, Let the Lord be magnified who has pleasure in the **prosperity** of your servant (Psalm 35:27, ULKJV.) Your cause is your kingdom, your glory and your covenant – the Gospel, and you **prosper** me for I favor your righteous cause.

I shall remember the reason you give me the **power to get wealth** – that it is to confirm your Covenant (Deuteronomy 8:18,) firstly to keep your promises and secondly to spread the Covenant – the New Covenant the Gospel about the Message of atonement through Jesus Christ around the world.[51]

Therefore, I shall partner with the Gospel in accordance with the principles of **giving and receiving**. As I support the Gospel, fruit will **abound** to my account. My **giving** to the work of the Lord is a sweet smell, a sacrifice acceptable, well-pleasing to God. And my

[51] Author's exhortation based on Deuteronomy 8:18, Matthew 28:19, Matthew 24:14.

God shall **supply** all my need according to his **riches** in glory by Christ Jesus (Philippians 4:15-18, ULKJV.)

Like Joanna, the wife of Chuza, Herod's chief house-servant, manager, administrator and steward, and like Susanna and a number of others, who gave unto Jesus of their **wealth and substance** for his needs (Luke 8:3, ULKJV, BBE, ISV,) so I too can liberally and **richly** financially support into the expansion of the kingdom of God and the message of Jesus Christ.

I pray and proclaim all of your promises in the most holy and most powerful name of the Lord Jesus Christ, Amen.

Abba – Father

Dear Heavenly Father,

You are *Abba* Father – my Divine Daddy Romans 8:15, ULKJV.) Your Word teaches that I should ask, and it shall be given me; seek, and I shall find; knock, and it shall be opened unto me: For every one that asks receives; and he that seeks finds; and to him that knocks it shall be opened. For you said what man is there of us, whom if his son asks bread, will he give him a stone? Or if he asks a fish, will he give him a serpent? And Lord Jesus, you said, If you all then, being evil, know how to give good gifts unto your children, how much more shall your Father which is in heaven give good things to them that ask him? (Matthew 7:11, ULKJV.)

And it is true: If imperfect people know how to give good gifts to their children, how much more will my heavenly Father give good gifts to those who ask him (NLT)? I praise you oh God: You are my Father, and you care for me more than any earthly father can. Your care for me is infinite and your love cannot be measured. And you will give good gifts to me for I ask this of you.[52]

Therefore, I taste and see that you are good, and **blessed** is the man that trusts in you (Psalm 34:8, ULKJV.) Lord you are good and I trust in you and I shall be **blessed**. For every good gift and every perfect gift is from above, and comes down from the Father of lights, with whom is no variableness, neither shadow of turning (James 1:17, ULKJV.) With you there is no variation or shifting shadow (NASB) and no inconsistency, (ISV.) You are my Father and you do not change for you said, I am the LORD, I change not (Malachi 3:6, ULKJV.)

I love you Father, thank you that you never change, and that you care for me.

I pray and proclaim all of your promises in the most holy and most powerful name of the Lord Jesus Christ, Amen.

---

[52] Author's exhortation based on Matthew 7:11.

Wealth and Riches

Father God, you are El Shaddai – the God of Plenty, the All Sufficient One, God Almighty, and the God of more than enough[53] (Genesis 17:1, ULKJV.) You are also Jehovah Jireh, - the **LORD my Provider**[54] (Genesis 22:14, ULKJV.) Today I lay claim to **wealth and riches** as is promised in your Word. All the promises of God are 'yes' and 'amen' in Christ Jesus, including the promises of **wealth and riches** (2 Corinthians 1:20, ULKJV.)

I praise you LORD, I am **blessed**, for **blessed is the man** that fears the LORD, that delights greatly in his commandments. My seed shall be mighty upon earth: the generation of the upright shall be **blessed**. **Wealth and riches** shall be in my house: and my righteousness endures for ever (Psalms 112:1-3, ULKJV.)

---

[53] The meaning of *El Shaddai.*
[54] The meaning of Jehovah Jireh

You give me **riches, wealth, and honor** (Ecclesiastes 6:2, ULKJV,) and you give me the ability to **enjoy all things richly** (1 Timothy 6:17, ULKJV.) You give me **riches and wealth**, and the power to eat thereof, and to take my portion. I rejoice in my labor; this is the gift of God (Ecclesiastes 5:19, ULKJV.) I love and seek your wisdom and **with your wisdom are** riches **and honor, enduring wealth** and **prosperity** (Proverbs 8:18, NIV.)

Because I seek your wisdom, **you crown me with riches** (Proverbs 14:24, ULKJV.) Length of days is in wisdom's right hand; and in her left hand **riches and honor** (Proverbs 3:16, ULKJV.) By wisdom and understanding **my chambers are filled with all precious and pleasant riches** (Proverbs 24:4, ULKJV.)

I seek your kingdom first, and **all these things shall be added unto me** (Matthew 6:33, ULKJV.) Because I seek your kingdom first you also give me **wealth, riches and honor** (2 Chronicles 1:12, ULKJV.)

My children will inherit **houses and wealth** from their parents, and **you will bless them** with prudent spouses (Proverbs 19:14, NIV.) I leave an inheritance to my children's children and the **wealth** of the sinner is laid up for the just (Proverbs 13:22, ULKJV.) My children, grandchildren, great grandchildren and my offspring for perpetual generations are **blessed** because of me – because of the God that I serve.

I feed on the **wealth** of nations, and in their **riches** I will boast (Isaiah 61:6, NIV.) I will be greater than my ungodly peers in **riches** and wisdom (2 Chronicles 9:22, ULKJV.) I have so much **riches**, so much **cattle, silver, gold, brass, iron, and raiment** that I can share it with my brethren (Joshua 22:8, ULKJV.)

In all this, I maintain **a good name**, which is rather to be chosen than **great riches**, and loving favor rather than silver and gold (Proverbs 22:1, ULKJV.)

Because I trust in the LORD and not in my riches, I shall not fall, but be as the righteous that will **flourish** as a branch (Proverbs 11:28, ULKJV.) You promise me **riches** in this world, but riches will not cause me to be high-minded, nor trust in uncertain riches, but in you, the living God, who gives to us **richly** all things to enjoy (1 Timothy 6:17, ULKJV.) I will indeed enjoy that which you give unto me **richly**.

When my **riches increase**, I do not set my heart or depend on them (Psalms 62:10, ULKJV & GWT.) I can have money without the love of money but with the love of God. I can **have wealth** but not trust in wealth, but in God. I can have **riches**, yet not trust in riches, but in the Living God, **who gives me all things richly to enjoy** (1 Timothy 6:17, ULKJV.) For if I trust in riches, it is easier for a camel to go through the eye of a needle, than for me to enter into the kingdom of God (Mark 10:23-25, ULKJV.) Therefore, I seek

God's kingdom first, and **all these things will be added unto me** (Matthew 6:33, ULKJV.) All the things that the Gentiles seek, for my heavenly Father knows that I have need of all these things (Matthew 6:32, ULKJV.)

Lord, you would that I was either cold or hot because you will spew the lukewarm out of your mouth. I will not be as those who say, I am rich, and increased with goods, and have need of nothing; and know not that they are wretched, and miserable, and poor, and blind, and naked: I buy of your **gold tried in the fire, that I may be rich**; and white raiment, that I may be clothed, and that the shame of my nakedness do not appear; and anoint mine eyes with eye salve, that I may see (Revelation 3:15-18, ULKJV.)

I do not *love* money or wealth, for the love of money is the root of all evil (1 Timothy 6:17, ULKJV,) rather I love you my God, and because I love you and because my affections are focused on you, you add all these things unto me (Matthew 6:33, ULKJV,) and you give me the **power to get wealth** (Deuteronomy 8:18, ULKJV.) Whoever loves money never has money enough; whoever loves wealth is never satisfied with his income (Ecclesiastes 5:10.)

I thank you my Father, that you bless me with money, as well as the things that money cannot buy.[55] If one were to give all the

[55] Author's exhortation

wealth of his house for love, it would be utterly scorned (Song of Solomon 8:7, NIV.)

Money can buy lust, but not love (Song of Solomon 8:7, ULKJV.) Money can buy medicine, but it cannot buy health. Money can buy a house, but not a home.[56] Money can buy companionship, but not friendship. Money can buy entertainment, but not happiness. Money can buy food, but not an appetite. Money can buy a bed, but not sleep. The sleep of a laboring man is sweet, whether he eat little or much: but the abundance of the rich will not suffer him to sleep (Ecclesiastes 5:12, ULKJV.) Money can buy religion but not salvation. Money can buy a crucifix, but not a savior. Jesus, you are my Savior, for the preaching of the cross is to them that perish foolishness; but unto us which are saved it is the power of God (1 Corinthians 1:18, ULKJV.)

I will not lay up treasures upon this earth and not be **rich** towards God (Luke 12:21, ULKJV.) However, **riches and honor in abundance** come my way (2 Chronicles 17:5, ULKJV.)

I will be enterprising and hardworking, for he becomes poor that deals with a slack hand: but **the hand of the diligent makes rich** (Proverbs 10:4, ULKJV.)

[56] Exhortation by the author – source unknown. Compare www.quotationsbook.com/quote/27210

I shall remember the LORD my God, that it is He that gives to me **power to get wealth** (Deuteronomy 8:18, ULKJV.)

I pray and proclaim all of your promises in the most holy and most powerful name of the Lord Jesus Christ, Amen.

Wealthy Servants of God

Father God,

Your Word teaches that there is no respect of persons with you (Colossians 3:25, ULKJV,) that you show no favoritism (NIV,) no partiality (NASB,) do things without respect for any man's position (BBE,) for with you there are no merely earthly distinctions (WNT.) Therefore, I can confidently thank you that you make no distinction between me and any other person you have **blessed**. I rejoice in their **blessing**, because as they have been **blessed**, so too shall I be **blessed**.

I thank you that you are indeed not a respecter of persons, and as you **blessed** someone else, so you will bless me too.[57]

---

[57] Author's exhortation. Of course God works uniquely in our different lives. Our lives unfold differently, and there is more than meets the eye than what the Scriptures invoked here may express. For example, God may materially bless some individuals in modern days as He had blessed these

You will bless me as you **blessed** Abraham, for Abram was very **rich in cattle, in silver, and in gold** (Genesis 13:2, ULKJV.) You bless me and make my name great, and I shall be a **blessing** (Genesis 12:2, ULKJV.) I will not only be **blessed** but I will be **blessed** to the point of being a **blessing!**[58]

You will **bless them that bless me** and curse them that curse me (Genesis 12:2-3, ULKJV)[59]. Our substance is so great, that the land is not able to bear us (Genesis 13:6, NIV.) I will not rely on man for my provision, or take from them as much as a thread or a shoe latchet, lest they say that they have made me rich (Genesis 14:23, ULKJV,) for it is the **blessing of the LORD that makes rich** (Proverbs 10:22, ULKJV,) not man.

As Eliezer said of Abraham, so it will be said of me, that the LORD has **blessed me greatly**, and that I have become great, and that God has given me **flocks, herds, silver, gold, menservants, maidservants, camels and asses** (Genesis 24:35, ULKJV.) When I send someone on an errand, I send them with **ample supply** to accomplish their task (Genesis 24:22.)

Bible examples of wealthy individuals his unique purposes, and may bless others in different ways. However, the author's intent is to encourage the reader to dare to believe that God will bless you as He has blessed the Bible characters referred to here.

[58] Author's exhortation based on Genesis 12:22.

[59] The blessing of Abraham has come upon the Gentiles through Jesus Christ (Galatians 3:14, ULKJV.)

As Isaac did, I too **prosper** even during a time of famine, because **you bless me**. I sow in the land, and receive in the same year **a hundredfold and you bless me** (Genesis 26:12, ULKJV.) I wax great, and go forward, and grow until I become very great (Genesis 26:13, ULKJV.) You bless me with such material **abundance**, that the Philistines envy me (Genesis 26:14, ULKJV.) My **wealth becomes very great, increasing more and more** (Genesis 26:13, BBE.) I am **enriched**, and I go on **prospering** and **increasing**, till I become **exceeding great** (Genesis 26:13, DRB.) I am so **blessed**, that I provoke jealousy from those who are not in covenant with you, for the Philistines became jealous of him (Genesis 26:14, GWT.) The roles are being reversed. Instead of God's covenant people envying the world, the world envies God's covenant people.[60] The nations call me **blessed** and a delightsome land (Malachi 3:12, ULKJV.)

Like Jacob did, I also receive my **prosperity** and **increase** directly from the LORD. I **increase exceedingly** (Genesis 30:43, ULKJV.) I become **exceedingly prosperous** and come to own large flocks, and maidservants and menservants, and camels and donkeys (Genesis 30:43, NIV.)

---

[60] Author's exhortation based on this Scripture.

I am not worthy of the least of all the mercies, and of all the truth, which you have shown unto your servant; for with my staff I passed over this Jordan; and now I am become two bands (Genesis 32:10, ULKJV.) Lord like Jacob, I too am desperate and determined to receive your **blessing**. I will not let you go, except you bless me (Genesis 32:26, ULKJV.) You change my nature and character as you did for Jacob when he became Israel. I have the nature of the Israel of God and I am a prince and conqueror with God (Genesis 32:28.) As a prince I have power with God and with men, and I prevail (Genesis 32:28, ULKJV,) and in my fight with God and with men I have overcome (Genesis 32:28, BBE.)

Like Jabez, I too call on the God of Israel, saying, Oh that you would **bless me indeed**, and enlarge my coast, and that your hand might be with me, and that you would keep me from evil, that it may not grieve me! And God grants me that which I request (1 Chronicles 4:10, ULKJV.)

As Job owned 7,000 sheep and goats, 3,000 camels, 1,000 oxen, 500 donkeys, and a large number of servants and was the most influential (Job 1:3, GWT,) the greatest of all the men in the east (ULKJV,) so too I shall be **wealthy** and **blessed** and be the greatest person in my sphere of influence. I will not allow fear to bring calamity upon me for fear placed Job into the hand of satan (Genesis 2:6; 3:25.) And though I may not understand the reason for my trials, for many are the afflictions (ULKJV,) or the adversities of the righteous, yet Jehovah delivers me out of them all (Psalms 34:19—DBY.) The LORD turns my captivity (ULKJV,) restores my fortunes..., the LORD **increases** all that I have twofold (Job 42:10, NASB,) and the LORD blesses the latter part of my life more than the first (Job 42:12, NIV.)

As Joseph, the **rich** man from Arimathaea had been a disciple of Jesus, I too shall be considered a **rich** person from my region, and a loyal, sold out disciple of Jesus, my Lord and Savior (Matthew 27:57.)

Like Joanna, the wife of Chuza, Herod's chief house-servant, manager, administrator and steward, and Susanna and a number of others, who gave unto Jesus of their **wealth** and substance for his needs (Luke 8:3, ULKJV, BBE, ISV,) so I too can liberally and **richly** financially support into the expansion of the kingdom of God and the message of Jesus Christ.

I pray and proclaim all of your promises in the most holy and most powerful name of the Lord Jesus Christ, Amen.

The Power to get Wealth

My Father God and Lord Jesus Christ,

In your Word you clearly promise unto your children **wealth** and **prosperity**. Today I call that **wealth** into my life by faith and prayer. Like my God, I call the things that be not as though they were (Romans 4:17, ULKJV.) Even if I do not see it right away, it doesn't change the way I believe. For my faith is based upon your Word, not upon the circumstances around me. I walk by faith and not by sight (2 Corinthians 5:7, ULKJV.)

I hold tightly without wavering to the hope we affirm, for God can be trusted to keep his promise (Hebrews 10:23, NLT.)

For God is not a man, that he should lie, nor a son of man, that he should change his mind. Does he speak and then not act? Does he promise and not fulfill? (Numbers 23:19, NIV.) With persistence I keep on coming until the answers to my prayers are manifested (Luke 18:1-8.)

Your Word promises that you will give me **power to get wealth**: I shall remember the LORD my God, that it is He that gives to me **power to get wealth** (Deuteronomy 8:18, ULKJV.) Amen, you give me **power to get wealth**, **riches** and substance.[61] I believe your Word, the whole Word and nothing but the Word, for your Word is truth (John 17:17, ULKJV.)

You give me the **power to get wealth** (Deuteronomy 8:18, ULKJV.) I have charge of, furnish, gather and maintain **wealth**, to go about and govern **wealth**. You cause me to be industrious, prepare, procure, and **provide wealth**.[62]

I know that **wealth** is not only the material things we possess. The **wealth** of God is primarily the spiritual **riches** we have in Christ Jesus, unfathomable **riches** of Christ (Ephesians 3:8, NASB,) the unending **wealth** of Christ (Ephesians 3:8, BBE,) attaining to all the **wealth** that comes from the full assurance of understanding, resulting in a true knowledge of God's mystery, that is, Christ Himself (Colossians 2:2, NASB.)

Like Moses did, I too esteem the reproach of Christ greater **riches** than the treasures in Egypt (Hebrews 11:26, ULKJV,) and trust not in uncertain **riches**, but in the Living God, who gives to us all

---

[61] Strong's Hebrew word # 2428 *chayil.*
[62] Strong's Hebrew word # 6213: *asah.*

things **richly** to enjoy (1 Timothy 6:17, ULKJV,) which includes not only spiritual, but also material **wealth** (Deuteronomy 8:18.)

I have gone through fire and through water: but you brought me out into a **wealthy place** (Psalms 66:12, ULKJV,) a **place of abundance** (Psalms 66:12, NIV,) and to **a place of satisfaction, running over and being wealthy**.[63]

You allow me to go through periods of fire and water to prove and try me as silver is tried (Psalms 66:10, ULKJV.) After you have tried me, I shall come forth as gold (Job 23:10, ULKJV.) That the trial of my faith, being much more precious than of gold that perishes, though it be tried with fire, might be found unto praise and honor and glory at the appearing of Jesus Christ (1 Peter 1:7, ULKJV.)

Therefore, I consent to it that you test me and put me through trials (Job 23:10, Psalms 66:10,) that I may come to **my wealthy place** (Psalms 66:12,) both spiritually and materially. [64]

When I go through a wilderness, I understand that you are humbling me, and proving me, that I may know what is in my heart, whether I would keep your commandments or not. You humble me and suffer me to hunger, and feed me with manna, which I knew not, that you may make me know that man does not live by bread only,

---

[63] Strong's Hebrew word # 7311 *ruwm*.
[64] Author's exhortation.

but by every word that proceeds out of the mouth of the LORD does man live…you bring me into a good land, a land of brooks of water, of fountains and depths that spring out of valleys and hills; a land of wheat, and barley, and vine, and fir trees, and pomegranates; a land of oil olive, and honey; a land wherein I eat bread without scarceness, and I do not lack any thing in it; a land whose stones are iron, and out of whose hills I may dig brass (Deuteronomy 8:2-9, ULKJV.)

When I have eaten and I'm full, then I shall bless the LORD my God for the good land which you have given me. I will beware that I forget not the LORD my God, in not keeping your commandments, and your judgments, and your statutes… (Deuteronomy 8:10-11, ULKJV.)

Lest when I have eaten and I'm full, and have built **goodly [and beautiful** (ISV)] **houses**, and dwelt therein; And when my herds and my flocks **multiply**, and my silver and my gold is multiplied, and all that I have is multiplied; then my heart being lifted up and I forget LORD my God… (Deuteronomy 8:12-14, ULKJV,) and say in my heart, that my power and the might of my hand has gotten me this **wealth** (Deuteronomy 8:17, ULKJV.)

But I shall remember you, oh LORD my God: for it is you that gives to me **power to get wealth**, that you may establish your covenant… (Deuteronomy 8:18, ULKJV.)

I shall not say unto myself that my power and the strength of my hands have produced this **wealth** for me. But I shall remember you, Lord my God, for it is you who gives the ability to produce **wealth**, and so confirm your covenant (Deuteronomy 8:17-18, NIV.)

You do not discourage me from being **wealthy**. The issue is that I remember Him who gave me the power produce the **wealth.**[65] I shall always remember that it is you, Yahweh my God, who gives me **power to get wealth** (Deuteronomy 8:18, WEB.)

I shall put my trust in you, the Living God, who gives me **all things richly to enjoy** (1 Timothy 6:17, ULKJV.)

I pray and proclaim all of your promises in the most holy and most powerful name of the Lord Jesus Christ, Amen.

---

[65] Author's exhortation.

Never Defeated

Heavenly Father,

I believe all your promises are 'yes' and 'amen' in Christ Jesus (1 Corinthians 1:20.) My faith is not merely based on the experiences of life, but on your Word, for heaven and earth shall pass away, but your Word shall not pass away (Mark 13:31, ULKJV.) Forever oh LORD is your Word settled in heaven (Psalm 119:89, ULKJV,) and it stands firm in the heavens (NIV.)

Therefore, I refuse to be defeated because I believe your Word and not the circumstances and trials of life.

Thanks be to God, which always causes me to triumph. (2 Corinthians 2:14, ULKJV) and always causes me to walk in triumphal procession (NIV.) You always lead me to victory (GWT.) And since you always, yes always cause me to triumph I know that I am and shall be victorious in my current circumstance. I refuse to be defeated.[66]

I pray and shall not faint (Luke 18:1, ULKJV.) I shall not lose heart (ESV) and never give up (NLT.) Any thing whatsoever I desire, when I pray, I believe that I receive *them*, and I shall have *them* (Mark 11:24, ULKJV.) I believe I have received it (NIV) and I will persist in prayer and faith until it is manifested in the natural realm.[67]

Like the widow who kept troubling (Luke 18:5, ULKJV) and bothering the judge (NIV) and wore him out by her continual coming (NASB), so God will avenge his own elect which cry day and night unto Him, though He bear long with them (Luke 18:7, ULKJV.) Nevertheless, you will avenge me speedily, but when the Son of Man comes, shall He find faith in the earth (Luke 18:8, ULKJV.) You will execute justice and vindicate[68] me speedily. Won't God grant his chosen people justice when they cry out to him day and night? Is he slow to help them (Luke 18:7—ISV)? And will not God avenge the wrongs of his Own People who cry aloud to Him day and night, although He seems slow in taking action on their behalf (WNT.)

Against hope, I believe in hope … according to that which was spoken. And being not weak in faith, I consider not [any

---

[66] Author's exhortation.
[67] Author's exhortation.
[68] Strong's Greek words for *avenge*: # 4060 and 1557.

outward evidence on the contrary[69]], and I stagger not at the promise of God through unbelief; but I am strong in faith, giving glory to God; And being fully persuaded that, what you have promised, you are able also to perform (Romans 4:18-21, ULKJV.)

I hope in spite of hopeless circumstances (ISV) and in utterly hopeless circumstances I hopefully believe (WNT.) The things which are seen were not made of things which do appear (Hebrews 11:3, ULKJV,) and these things that are seen came into being out of those things which are unseen (ABPE.)

By faith I understand that the world was framed by the word of God; that from invisible things visible things might be made (Hebrews 11:3, DRB.) The universe has been framed by the word of God, so that what is seen has not been made out of things which are visible (WEB,) so too I shall not be discouraged and defeated when I do not see the manifestation of my **provision** in the natural.[70] The revelation awaits an appointed time; it speaks of the end and will not prove false. Though it lingers, I wait for it; it will certainly come and will not delay (Habakkuk 2:3, NIV.)

---

[69] Author's exhortation: In Abraham's case it was his "dead body" and the "deadness of Sarah's womb" that was the external contrary evidence that did not rhyme with God's promises. In our case we may have similar adversarial circumstances, but just like Abraham made God's promises manifest into reality by his faith, so we do the same.)

[70] Author's exhortation based on Hebrews 11:3.

God, you are not a man, that you should lie, nor a son of man, that you should change your mind. Would you speak and then not act? Would you promise and not fulfill (Numbers 23:19, NIV)? Rather, what you promised you are able also to perform (Romans 4:21, ULKJV) and I am absolutely certain that whatever promise you are bound by, you are able also to make good (WNT.)

I pray and proclaim all of your promises in the most holy and most powerful name of the Lord Jesus Christ, Amen.

Superior Spiritual Riches

Father God, I acknowledge today that the **spiritual riches** that come from you is greater than the riches this world has to offer. Therefore, I affirm today that I value the things of the Spirit more than the things of this world. [71]

For they that are after the flesh do mind the things of the flesh; but they that are after the Spirit the things of the Spirit. For to be carnally minded is death; but to be spiritually minded is life and peace. But the carnal mind is enmity against God: for it is not subject to the law of God, neither indeed can be. So then they that are in the flesh cannot please God. But I am not in the flesh, but in the Spirit, if so be that the Spirit of God dwell in me. (Romans 8:5-9, ULKJV.)

---

[71] Author's exhortation based on the Scriptures used in this prayer.

My life does not consist in the abundance of the things that I possess (Luke 12:15, ULKJV.) Rather, I revel in the **spiritual riches** I have in Christ Jesus, the unfathomable **riches of Christ** (Ephesians 3:8, NASB,) and the unending **wealth** of Christ (BBE.)

Therefore, I shall not only be rich in the world but void of God, for woe unto them that are rich! for they have received their consolation. Woe unto them that are full! for they shall hunger (Luke 6:24-25, NIV.) [72]

Rather, I am **rich towards God**, and place my affections on your kingdom first, and all these things shall be added unto me (Matthew 6:33, ULKJV.) I shall **be full and have plenty of bread and provision** (Proverbs 20:13, Proverbs 28:19, Proverbs 12:11, Proverbs 27:27, Psalms 78:25, 1 Chronicles 12:40, Isaiah 33:16, ULKJV.)

---

[72]"There was a rich man who was dressed in purple and fine linen and lived in luxury every day. At his gate was laid a beggar named Lazarus, covered with sores and longing to eat what fell from the rich man's table. Even the dogs came and licked his sores.
The time came when the beggar died and the angels carried him to Abraham's side. The rich man also died and was buried. In hell, where he was in torment, he looked up and saw Abraham far away, with Lazarus by his side. So he called to him, 'Father Abraham, have pity on me and send Lazarus to dip the tip of his finger in water and cool my tongue, because I am in agony in this fire. But Abraham replied, 'Son, remember that in your lifetime you received your good things, while Lazarus received bad things, but now he is comforted here and you are in agony. And besides all this, between us and you a great chasm has been fixed, so that those who want to go from here to you cannot, nor can anyone cross over from there to us.' He answered, 'Then I beg you, father, send Lazarus to my father's house, for I have five brothers. Let him warn them, so that they will not also come to this place of torment.' Abraham replied, 'They have Moses and the Prophets; let them listen to them.' No, father Abraham,' he said, 'but if someone from the dead goes to them, they will repent.' He said to him, 'If they do not listen to Moses and the Prophets, they will not be convinced even if someone rises from the dead..." (Luke 16:19-31, NIV.)

The greatest **riches** are **spiritual riches**—when I am **rich** towards God (Luke 12:21, ULKJV.)

I count all things but loss for the excellency of the knowledge of Christ Jesus my Lord[73]: for whom I have suffered the loss of all things, and do count them but dung, that I may win Christ, and be found in you and know you (Philippians 3:8-10, ULKJV.)

I esteem the reproach of Christ **greater riches** than the treasures in Egypt (Hebrews 11:26, ULKJV,) and trust not in uncertain riches, but in the Living God, who **gives to us all things richly to enjoy** (1 Timothy 6:17, ULKJV.)

I attain to all the **wealth** that comes from the full assurance of understanding, resulting in a true knowledge of God's mystery, that is, Christ Himself (Colossians 2:2, NASB.) Christ in me, the hope of glory (Colossians 1:27, ULKJV.)[74]

I value the **prosperity** of my soul more than that of my natural surroundings, but I thank you Lord that you also bless me with **prosperity** and health even as my soul **prospers**, for your Word says that for as your beloved, you wish above all things that I

---

[73] See author's book *The Wonder of Jesus* for an uplifting detailed study of the Jesus Christ – God in the Flesh.
[74] See author's book *Manifesting Christ in you* for great truths regarding the indwelling of Christ within the believer.

may **prosper** and be in health, even as my soul **prospers** (3 John 2, ULKJV.)

Oh Father, I pray and I declare all these truths and Scriptures in the mighty and holy Name of Jesus Christ, (John 16:23,) and I ask and I shall receive, that my joy may be full (John 16:24, ULKJV,) Amen.

No Lack

Oh God,

You are *Jehovah Rohi* – The LORD my Shepherd, and I shall not want (Psalm 23:1, ULKJV.) I have all that I need (NLT), I am never in need (GWT) and I shall lack nothing (ABPE.)

The young lions do lack, and suffer hunger, but those who seek Yahweh shall not lack any good thing (Psalm 34:10 WEB.) I have all the good things I need (GWT.)

I trust in the LORD, and I do good; so shall I dwell in the land, and verily I shall be fed. I delight myself also in the LORD; and he shall give me the desires of my heart (Psalm 37:3-4, ULKJV.) You grant me my requests and petitions,[75] and the desires of my heart.

[75] Strong's Hebrew word #4863: *mishalot.*

Like Jabez, I also I call on the God of Israel, saying, Oh that you would bless me indeed, and enlarge my coast, and that your hand might be with me, and that you would keep me from evil, that it may not grieve me! And God, you grant me that which I request (1 Chronicles 4:10, ULKJV.)

I shall eat bread without scarceness, I shall not lack any thing in it; a land whose stones are iron, and out of whose hills I may dig brass. When I have eaten and am full, then I shall bless the LORD my God for the good land (the good life)[76] which he has given me (Deuteronomy 8:9-10, ULKJV.)

The silver *is* yours, and the gold *is* yours, oh LORD of hosts, (Haggai 2:8, ULKJV,) and you own the cattle on a thousand hills (Psalm 50:10 ULKJV.)

With you there is no lack nor scarcity, and you provide for me.

I pray and proclaim all of your promises in the most holy and most powerful name of the Lord Jesus Christ, Amen.

---

[76] Author exhortation: Inserted the words "the good life" to remain relevant to how God's blessings apply to us individually and to us as the Body of Christ.

Overtaken with Blessings

Father God, I thank you today for your many **blessings and promises**, and that all your promises in Christ *are* 'yes', and in him 'amen,' unto the glory of God by us (2 Corinthians 1:20, ULKJV.) For no matter how many promises God has made, they are 'yes' in Christ. And so through him the 'amen' is spoken by us to the glory of God (NIV.) For all the promises of God find their 'yes' in you. That is why it is through you that I utter my 'amen' to God for 'your' glory (ISV.)

God, I confirm it verbally and by faith and I proclaim my 'amen' on these **blessings** that shall come on me and overtake me if I shall hearken[77] unto the voice of the LORD my God:

---

[77] "Hearken" includes observing, doing, and not going aside from any of the words that He commands us to the right hand or to the left, to go after other gods to serve them (Deuteronomy 28:1, 14.)

Blessed shall I be in the city, and **blessed** shall I be in the field. Blessed shall be the fruit of my body, and the fruit of my ground, and the fruit of my cattle, the **increase** of my herd, and the flocks of my sheep. **Blessed** shall be my basket and my store. **Blessed** shall I be when I come in and **blessed** shall I be when I go out. The LORD shall cause my enemies that rise up against me to be smitten before my face: they shall come out against me one way, and flee before me seven ways. You shall command the **blessing** upon me in my storehouses, and in all that I set my hand unto; and you shall bless me in the land which the LORD my God gives to me…

You make me **plenteous in goods**… and you open unto me your good treasure, the heaven to give the rain unto my land in his season, and you **bless** all the work of my hand; and I shall lend unto many nations, and I shall not borrow. You make me the head and not the tail; and I shall be above only and not beneath (Deuteronomy 28:2-13, ULKJV.)

Any thing whatsoever I desire, when I pray, I believe that I receive *them*, and I shall have *them* (Mark 11:24, ULKJV.) Therefore, I pray that these **blessings shall overtake me** and that I will be the **possessor of these blessings** that I ask from God, and that you oh God yourself have promised unto me.

I am willing and obedient, and I shall eat the good (even the best, NIV) of the land (Isaiah 1:19, ULKJV.) I am willing and have hearkened, the good of the land I shall consume (YLT.)

I pray and proclaim all of your promises in the most holy and most powerful name of the Lord Jesus Christ, Amen.

Prayer of Salvation (Shorter Version)

You may pray this following prayer as a guideline:

"Dear God. I am a sinner. I cannot save myself. I need a Savior, and Your Name is Jesus. Thank You God that You came to earth to reach me and to save me. Forgive me of all my sin and wash me clean with the precious blood of Jesus,

I believe with my heart and confess with my mouth that Jesus died and rose again. I further declare that Jesus is my Lord from this day forward forever. You are my only God.

I open my life to you. Lord Jesus, come live in my heart. Please give me the power of Your Spirit that I may live righteously. Thank You for giving me eternal life, and that when I die I will meet Jesus and live in heaven with You forever.

Amen.

Prayer of Salvation (Longer Version)

God's **blessings** are for his children, so we should make sure that we accept or reaffirm our faith in Jesus Christ and in God as our Father.[78] If you want to receive Jesus Christ as your Lord and Savior, pray this prayer with all your heart:

Oh God, I come to you today in the Name of Jesus.

I confess that I am a sinner. I am not worthy to even lift up my eyes to heaven. Have mercy on me, a sinner. I know that I cannot save myself, and therefore I need a Savior. For the wages of sin is

---

[78] Man should not pray the prayer of salvation for the selfish reason of wanting to merely receive God's many blessings. Rather, the gift of God is eternal life through Christ Jesus our Lord (Romans 6:23.) We accept Christ in response to his grace and the free gift of eternal life. For by grace are you all saved through faith; and that not of yourselves: *it is* the gift of God (Ephesians 2:8.) This in itself is the most wonderful thing ever. But the side benefits of accepting Christ is that by doing so we come into covenant with God. He is our God and we are his people, and you become his child. From this covenant relationship we have the humble right to receive the blessings as outlined in his Word.

death but the gift of God is eternal life through Jesus Christ our Lord (Romans 6:23, ULKJV.) There is only one God and one Mediator between God and men, the man Christ Jesus; Who gave himself a ransom for all… (1 Timothy 2:5, ULKJV.) Therefore, I accept and reaffirm that Jesus Christ is my Lord and Savior.

I confess with my mouth and I believe with my heart that Jesus is Lord, that He died for my sins and rose from the dead. For with the heart man believes unto righteousness; and with the mouth confession is made unto salvation (Romans 10:9-10, ULKJV.) With man it is impossible, but not with God, for with God all things are possible (Matthew 19:26, ULKJV.)

Lord Jesus, you stand at the door. I hear your voice and open the door, you come in and sup with me and me with you (Revelation 3:20, ULKJV.) I open the door to you by faith. Come into my heart and into my life. I surrender every part of my being to you, and I ask that your Spirit dwell within my body as in a temple, (1 Corinthians 3:16, ULKJV.)

For the preaching of the cross is to them that perish foolishness; but unto us which are saved it is the power of God (1 Corinthians 1:18, ULKJV.)[79] I don't place my faith in a crucifix, but

---

79 "For the message about the cross is nonsense to those who are being destroyed, but it is God's power to us who are being saved" (ISV.) "The message of the crucifixion is insanity to the lost, but to those of us who have life it is the power of God (ABPE.)

rather on the One who hung on that old rugged cross and in what He did for me on the cross.

I receive Jesus Christ into my life. To as many as receive you, you give power to become the sons and daughters of God, even to me that believe on your Name (John 1:12-13, ULKJV.) Father, I have been like a prodigal son or daughter, but I come to myself. Oh Father, I have sinned against heaven and before you. I am not worthy to be called your son or daughter. Yet today you have compassion on me, you run unto me, you fall on my neck and kiss me. You clothe me with the best robe and put a ring on my finger and shoes on my feet. You bring out the fatted calf, for your child was lost and now I am found (Luke 15:18-24, ULKJV.)

Thank you that you don't condemn me and therefore I will go and sin no more (John 8:11, ULKJV.) I repent of my sin and I am or shall be baptized in the Name of the Lord Jesus Christ for the remission of my sin and I shall receive the Holy Spirit (Acts 2:38, ULKJV.) I am or shall be baptized in the Name of the Father, and of the Son and of the Holy Ghost (Matthew 28:19, ULKJV.)

I ask that you give me power over sin. I walk in the Spirit and will not fulfill the lusts of the flesh (Galatians 5:16, ULKJV.) I cannot have victory over sin in my own strength. It is not by might nor by power, but by your Spirit that I am able to live victoriously over sin (Zechariah 4:6, ULKJV.)

Thank you Holy Spirit for becoming my Comforter, close companion and best friend (John 14:16-17, ULKJV.) Because I am a son or daughter of God, I will be led by the Spirit of God (Romans 8:14.) You dwell inside me, and greater is He that is in me than he that is in the world (1 John 4:4, ULKJV.)

I believe your Word is true. I believe God is not a man that He should lie or the son of man that He should repent. Shall He say something and not do it, or speak something and not make it good? (Numbers 23:19, ULKJV.) Your Word says that whoever comes to you, you will in no wise cast out (John 6:37, ULKJV), you will never reject me (NLT) and never turn me away (NLT.)

Therefore, I know that you have accepted me in the Beloved (Ephesians 1:6, ULKJV.) I am born again, I am born of water and of the Spirit (John 3:5, ULKJV), and I am born from above (John 3:5, NRSV.) Because I am in Christ, I am a new creation. The old things have passed away and all things have become new (2 Corinthians 5:17, ULKJV.)

He who has the Son has eternal life. Lord Jesus, because I have received you, I have also received eternal life (1 John 5:12, ULKJV.) I know that I have eternal life because I believe on the Name of the Son of God (1 John 5:13, ULKJV.)

I pray this in the Name of Jesus, and thank you for your goodness. Amen.

What to Do Now

Congratulations on receiving Jesus as your Lord and Savior! He now lives in your heart and you have received eternal life.

Now it is important that you grow in your faith and in your journey with God:

1. Tell several people that you have received Jesus Christ – not only will this one simple act give you a spiritual growth spurt, but it will give them an opportunity to receive Jesus too;
2. Be baptized by immersion, according to Matthew 28:19 and Acts 2:38 – in the Name of the Father, Son and Holy Spirit and in the Name of Jesus Christ;
3. Find a powerful, enthusiastic church that preaches the Bible without compromise, and attend it regularly;

4. Seek earnestly to be baptized in the Holy Spirit and power – which is a glorious experience accompanied by the speaking in tongues as in Acts 1:5-8 and 2:1-4;
5. Obtain a Bible (digital or paper,) and read it daily – if you read 3 chapters a day you will complete it in a year;
6. Pray daily – set aside a special time of your day for you and God, and also pray throughout the day (talk to God as if He's your friend;)
7. Refrain from old sinful habits like bad language and substance abuse – avoid the places and people who discourage your faith;
8. Make Christian friends that build you up and encourage you – they need you as much as you need them!

About the Author

Dr. Joel Hitchcock has been in the full time ministry for over 25 years as an evangelist and pastor.

Joel is married to Heidi and they have four children - Anthony, Rebekah, Timothy and Trey.

Joel has preached the Good News of Salvation, Healing and the Holy Spirit all around the world - in more than 45 countries. Multitudes have attended his mass evangelism miracle campaigns.

Joel has authored several full sized books such as:

- Son of God and Man – the Deity and Humanity of Jesus Christ;
- Christ in You – Union with God;
- The Miracle Ministry of Signs and Wonders;
- Mass Evangelism – the Power of City Wide Gospel Campaigns;

- Miracles for the Multitudes (Combination of the Miracle and Mass Evangelism books)
- God's Abundant Provision;
- Jehovah Incarnate – the Wonder of Jesus Christ;
- The Champion in You

Joel has also authored several smaller booklets such as:

- The Great King and the Little Ant;
- One Almighty Mediator; and
- When Jesus Moves into Your House

Joel also maintains several blogs, and has a growing YouTube ministry, such as:

- www.joelhitchcock.blogspot.com
- www.youtube.com/joelhitchcock

Having completed is doctoral thesis on *The Deity and Humanity of Jesus Christ,* Joel's great passion is centered around the Person of Jesus Christ, and our union with Him.

Photo Album

The primary reason to believe God for **prosperity** and **abundant provision** is to spread the Gospel. These pictures were taken at several of Joel and Heidi Hitchcock's evangelistic outreaches.

India

Venezuela

India

India

India

Uganda

Uganda

Venezuela

Venezuela

Venezuela

Venezuela

Dominican Republic

India

Pakistan

Joel Hitchcock at Reinhard Bonnke's CFAN Gospel Campaign

Cameroon

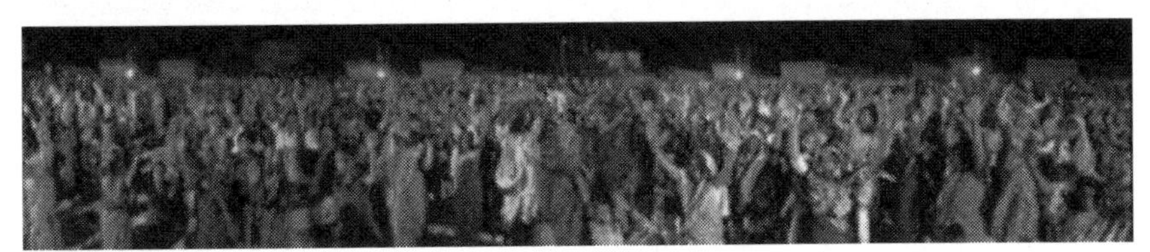

India

India

Delaware, USA

North Carolina, USA

India

Delaware, USA

India

Village in India

India

Maryland, USA

Joel Hitchcock Ministries Support

The main reason God wishes to bless you with **prosperity** and with financial **provision**, is not only to take care of you, but to enable you to support the work of God. It says, *"But seek you all first the kingdom of God, and his righteousness; and all these things shall be added unto you" (Matthew 6:33,* ULKJV.*)*

Joel Hitchcock Ministries is taking the Gospel around the world, and multitudes have come to Christ and have been healed in his Gospel campaigns. Consider becoming a supporter of Joel Hitchcock Ministries today!

➔ you may send a generous gift to Joel Hitchcock Ministries, PO Box 936, Georgetown DE 19947,

➔ you may give online at www.joelhitchcock.com,

➔ you may include Joel Hitchcock Ministries in your will,

➔ you may sponsor the printing of Joel Hitchcock's books, especially about the *Wonder of Jesus* and about *Manifesting Christ in you,*

➔ you may underwrite a Gospel Campaign for:

$50,000 (large city – about 100,000 people expected in attendance,) or

$25,000 (medium sized city – about 50,000 people expected in attendance,) or

$10,000 (small city - about 10,000 people expected in attendance.)

Joel Hitchcock Ministries is a non-profit 501 (C) 3 Evangelistic Corporation, registered with and reports annually to the Internal Revenue Service (Tax ID 51-038-6414.)

your gifts are tax deductible as allowed under the guidelines of the IRS code.

A Note on the Versions of the Bible

There are many translations and versions of the Bible, all trying to mirror its inerrancy as it is in the original languages. However, the King James Version of the Bible is undoubtedly one of the most accurate translations of the Bible from the languages in which the Bible originally was written. It has also been one of the most beloved translations in Christendom, which has stood the test of time.

Therefore, I have largely used the King James Version of the Bible in these prayers, updated some antiquated language (e.g. "which swath" to "that sows," "thou" to "you," "whithersoever" to "wherever," etc.) I created the acronym (ULKJV) for *Updated Language King James Version* –, whenever I updated such language from the King James Version.

I have also freely used several other translations of the Bible[80], and noted the version by its abbreviation, such as ASV for American Standard Version, NIV for New International Version, etc.

I also adapted it to sound more personalized in prayer form, such as, "Lord, it is your will that I **prosper** and are in health...," in stead of "Beloved, I wish above all things that you **prosper**..."

To emphasize the original meaning of some scriptures I have also freely used definitions from the Strong's Exhaustive Concordance[81] of Greek and Hebrew Words. To emphasize certain Bible words, I also occasionally used the Webster's[82] dictionary.

And though not as much, I also borrowed from perhaps a song or some other inspirational thoughts. In such instances I have inserted the reference in a footnote at the bottom of the page, as I have when I added or inserted my own exhortation. Such inspirational thoughts stand supportive to the Word of God, but it still remains in the very Word of God itself where the power and inspiration lays.

---

[80] BibleHub.com has been utilized for this purpose.
[81] Strong's Exhaustive Concordance, hereafter referred to as "Strong's".
[82] Merriam-Webster's 11th edition of the Collegiate Dictionary, hereafter referred to as "Webster's".

Scripture References

ULKJV: Most Bible references are taken from the King James Version (KJV) of the Bible, which the author has abbreviated as ULKJV wherever antiquated KJV language was updated. The author has also utilized other versions of the Bible, annotated in alphabetical order as follows:

ABPE: Aramaic Bible in Plain English, The Original Aramaic New Testament in Plain English- with Psalms & Proverbs. Copyright © 2007; 5th edition Copyright © 2010 - All rights reserved. Used by Permission.

AMP: Scripture quotations marked "AMP" are taken from the Amplified® Bible, Copyright © 1954, 1958, 1962, 1964, 1965, 1987 by The Lockman Foundation. Used by permission.

ASV: Scripture quotations marked "ASV" are taken from the American Standard Version Bible (Public Domain.)

BBE: Scripture quotations marked "BBE" are taken from the Bible in Basic English, printed in 1965 by Cambridge Press in England (Public domain.)

DBY: Scripture quotations marked "DBY" are taken from the Darby Translation Bible (Public Domain.)

DRB: Scripture quotations marked "DRB" are taken from the Douay-Rheims Bible (Public Domain.)

ESV: Scripture quotations marked "ESV" are from the ESV Bible® (The Holy Bible, English Standard Version®), copyright © 2001 by Crossway Bibles, a publishing ministry of Good News Publishers. Used by permission. All rights reserved.

GWT: GOD'S WORD is a copyrighted work of God's Word to the Nations. Scripture Quotations marked "God's Word" are used by permission. Copyright 1995 by God's Word to the Nations. Used by permission of Baker Publishing Group. All rights reserved.

GT: Goodspeed Translation, Edgard J Goodspeed, 1942.

ISV: International Standard Version® Release 2.1. Copyright © 1996-2012 The ISV Foundation. All rights reserved internationally.

NASB: Scripture quotations marked "NASB" are taken from the New American Standard Bible®, Copyright © 1960, 1962,

WNT: Weymouth New Testament (Public Domain.)

YLT: Young's Literal Translation (Public Domain.)

Emphases in italics or underlined text are that of the author's.

Contact Information

Joel Hitchcock Ministries,
PO Box 936, Georgetown DE 19947
United States of America

302-858-0887

www.joelhitchcock.blogspot.com
www.youtube.com/joelhitchcock
www.twitter.com/joelhitchcock
www.facebook.com/hitchcockjoel
www.jehovahincarnate.blogspot.com

35102757R00084

Made in the USA
Middletown, DE
04 February 2019